P9-AOW-335

SWIFT AND ANGLICAN
RATIONALISM

SWIFT AND ANGLICAN RATIONALISM

THE RELIGIOUS BACKGROUND OF
A TALE OF A TUB

Phillip Harth

THE UNIVERSITY OF CHICAGO PRESS

Chicago and London

LIBRARY OF CONGRESS CATALOG CARD NUMBER: 61-15934

THE UNIVERSITY OF CHICAGO PRESS, CHICAGO 60637
THE UNIVERSITY OF CHICAGO PRESS, LTD., LONDON W.C. I
© 1961 BY THE UNIVERSITY OF CHICAGO. ALL RIGHTS RESERVED
PUBLISHED 1961. SECOND IMPRESSION 1969
PRINTED IN THE UNITED STATES OF AMERICA

*To My Mother
and the Memory
of My Father*

CONTENTS

PREFACE

The major part of the research for this book was made possible by a Fulbright Award which relieved me from teaching duties and enabled me to spend two years at the British Museum. The Northwestern University Graduate School Committee on Research contributed funds for the typing of the manuscript.

I wish to thank the staffs of the British Museum and of Dr. Williams's Library, London, as well as those of the Newberry Library, Chicago, the Harper Library of the University of Chicago, and the Deering Library of Northwestern University for their helpful co-operation.

It is a pleasure to record here my thanks to Professors Jean H. Hagstrum, Zera S. Fink, and Walter B. Rideout of Northwestern University, who read the manuscript of this book and offered many helpful suggestions toward the improvement of its style.

My debt to Professors Ronald S. Crane and Arthur Friedman of the University of Chicago can never be adequately recorded. As teachers, they provided me with foundations without which I could not have written this book. As friends, they have offered me encouragement without which I would not have published it.

Last, I owe my wife thanks greater than those which it is customary to record in a preface. To read the manuscript of her husband's book is perhaps no more than is to be expected of any wife. To have read, as she has patiently done, every version of each page and to have contributed to the improvement of each is surely supererogatory.

Chapter 1

THE TWO BACKGROUNDS OF
A TALE OF A TUB

Where the performance of a writer is concerned, Johnson observed in the *Preface to Shakespeare,* "curiosity is always busy to discover the instruments, as well as to survey the workmanship, to know how much is to be ascribed to original powers, and how much to casual and adventitious help." There are relatively few works, viewed as artistic constructions, in which the "original powers" of the author — those internal circumstances of thought, feeling, and the like — have received none of the "adventitious help" provided by such external circumstances as the literary conventions of his time, the intellectual commonplaces shared by some at least of his contemporaries, and even those more particular aids to which we refer when we speak of an author's "sources." To the extent that any work is the product of both these sets of circumstances, neither can be ignored if we would form a just estimate of the author's achievement. It is only when we become aware of that complex of ideas, assumptions, and attitudes which the author owes to his predecessors and contemporaries that we are in a position to recognize and assess both kinds of originality which may appear in his work: that of inventing some of his materials and that, not less valuable, of putting conventional materials to new uses. But for this we need a knowledge, as specific as possible, of the background of the work.

I have attempted in this study to reconstruct such a background for Swift's religious satire in *A Tale of a Tub* by isolating those elements of thought and conventions of treatment which

Swift borrowed, showing the probable sources of these materials in the immediate background of the satire and analyzing the new and original uses to which he put them in the service of his specific satirical intention. At the same time, I have purposely ignored the non-religious satire in the *Tale*, on the grounds that this was the product of different circumstances and grew out of a background entirely distinct from that of the religious satire. It is not often, certainly, that a single book consists of two parts so completely separable, each of which can be traced to different origins. I shall begin, therefore, by reviewing some facts about the *Tale* which are scarcely novel but which have been ignored, nevertheless, in a recent attempt to show that there is unity of purpose and structure in Swift's book.[1]

A Tale of a Tub is a satire which deals with two separate subjects: abuses in religion and abuses in learning. Furthermore, these subjects are treated by the author, not separately and consecutively in two distinct halves, nor yet again simultaneously, but in a manner unique to this book: by an alternating pattern of sections which oscillates between the abuses in religion and the abuses in learning. This must have been obvious to the earliest readers of the book when it appeared in 1704, and Swift was merely confirming the obvious when, in the important "Apology" prefixed to the fifth edition of the *Tale* in 1710, he described the purpose and arrangement of his book:

> He thought the numerous and gross Corruptions in Religion and Learning might furnish Matter for a Satyr, that would be useful and diverting: He resolved to proceed in a manner, that should be altogether new, the World having been already too long nauseated with endless Repetitions upon every Subject. The Abuses in Religion he proposed to set forth in the Allegory of the Coats, and the three Brothers,

[1] See Ronald Paulson, *Theme and Structure in Swift's "Tale of a Tub"* (New Haven, Conn., 1960). Upon theoretical foundations supplied by Northrop Frye's *Anatomy of Criticism*, Mr. Paulson suggests that *A Tale of a Tub* deals with a unified theme (the "Gnostic myth" which serves as "archetype" for both the subjects of Swift's satire) and displays a unified structure (an "anatomy" of which the putative author in every section of the book is "the Hack"). I have discussed Mr. Paulson's method and conclusions in *Modern Philology*, LVIII (1961), 282–85.

which was to make up the Body of the Discourse. Those in Learning he chose to introduce by way of Digressions.[2]

The digressions which are entirely unrelated to the "body of the discourse" are Sections III ("A Digression concerning Criticks"), V ("A Digression in the Modern Kind"), VII ("A Digression in Praise of Digressions"), and X. These digressions, in addition to the greatest part of the prefatory material (including the "Dedication to Prince Posterity," "The Preface," and Section I, "The Introduction"), as well as "The Conclusion," all serve the same general purpose. Although apparently concerned with diverse subjects, these sections of the book all share the same satirical target: abuses in learning. And these abuses in learning are of a specific character, as becomes apparent as early as the "Dedication to Prince Posterity." They are the abuses of "modern learning" as seen and portrayed by an adherent of "ancient learning" in the famous quarrel over the relative merits of ancient and modern learning.

The "body of the discourse," as Swift called it, which contains his satire on abuses in religion, consists of Sections II, IV, VI, VIII, and XI, which relate the tale of the three brothers, and Section IX, "A Digression concerning the Original, the Use and Improvement of Madness in a Commonwealth." This last, although quite properly labeled a digression, is not at all a digression in the same sense as are the other sections which carry this designation. The other digressions each represent a structural break with the preceding section, abruptly interrupting the narrative in order to introduce some entirely different topic, which, it soon appears, is connected with modern learning. Section IX, on the other hand, is a digression of an altogether different sort. Structurally, it is intimately connected with Section VIII, which immediately precedes it. Section VIII, at this point in the narrative, has just presented a detailed examination of the beliefs and practices of the Aeolists, a sect founded by one of the three brothers, Jack. Before this, Section VI had related how Jack "had run out of his Wits."

[2] *The Prose Works of Jonathan Swift*, ed. Herbert Davis (Oxford, 1939—), I, 1. All quotations from Swift's prose works will be taken from this edition, which hereafter will be referred to by volume and page immediately following the quotation itself. Italics are to be understood for quotations from the "Apology."

3

Section IX, as the opening paragraph makes clear, is introduced to show that it is neither disgraceful nor exceptional that the sect described in the preceding section should have had a madman for its founder, since the authors of all "the greatest Actions that have been performed in the World" have been mad. Historical instances are offered in support of this assertion, followed by an extended analysis of the causes which account for the fact that all of these great actions, not the least of which was the establishment of the sect described in Section VIII, have originated in the madness of their authors. Section IX is a digression, then, but only in the sense that it interrupts the story of Jack's madness in order to discuss the genus of which Jack's disorder is a species. Thus Section IX is a logical outgrowth of Section VIII and serves as an appendix to it, since they both deal with the same subject, treated first in particular and then in general. That such was Swift's intention is indicated by the fact that Section X is a genuine digression, glancing off from the subject to treat an entirely different topic (modern learning), while Section XI returns, in keeping with Swift's habit of alternating the two satires, to the subject of Jack's later adventures.

Besides pointing out the purpose and arrangement of his book, the statement which I have quoted from the "Apology" also draws attention to the wholly different methods which Swift employs in his book for satirizing his two targets. His manner "that should be altogether new" was to consist in allegory for attacking the abuses in religion and in digression for ridiculing the abuses in learning. This is hardly a complete description of the satirical methods, so varied and so complex, which Swift employs against his targets, nor was it intended to be. Allegory is not the method of his religious satire in the "Digression concerning Madness," nor is digression the method of his satire on abuses in learning in the "Dedication to Prince Posterity," "The Preface," and "The Introduction." What Swift's distinction is intended to convey is the fact that the abuses in religion are treated in a manner appropriate to imaginary narrative, so that whether he is narrating the tale of the coat and the three brothers or interrupting his narration to relate a myth (as that of the tailor-worshippers in Section II or that of the Aeolists in Section VIII) or to discuss the genus "madness" of which Jack's disorder is a species (as he does in Section IX), he consistently preserves the "Character of an Historian" (I,

83). On the other hand, the abuses in learning are treated in a manner appropriate to an essay rather than to a narrative, and this second manner is consistently maintained wherever the abuses in learning are the subject, whether in those sections properly labeled "digressions" or in the prefatory material at the beginning of the book. Furthermore, as has been pointed out frequently in recent years, the essayist who treats the abuses in learning in this distinctive second manner is supposedly not Swift at all, but an impersonation of a "modern author." [3]

The essential feature of the impersonation in this second manner is not the mock-encomium which enables Swift, in the person of the imaginary modern author, to appear to praise those very characteristics of modern learning which it is his purpose to condemn. Mock-encomium may involve impersonation, as it does in *The Praise of Folly* or in Swift's satire on abuses in learning. But mock-encomium is also possible without any impersonation at all, as in numerous neo-Latin mock-encomia of the sixteenth century or in Swift's religious satire in Section IX of the *Tale*, where madness and madmen are certainly praised, but by a simple irony of inversion rather than by impersonation. What is really essential to the impersonation of Swift's second manner is that wherever it appears in any section of *A Tale of a Tub* we shortly become aware of three things: (1) the evocation of a distinct personality with hopes, plans, likes, dislikes, traits of character, a specific place of residence, and membership in a particular society; (2) the identification of this impersonated author with the moderns, so that he not only feels intense admiration for this group but is actually one of them himself; and (3) the use of this impersonated author as a surrogate for the targets of Swift's satire, so that they are unwittingly condemned by the laudatory excesses of one of their own group.

These three essential features of the impersonation in *A Tale of a Tub* are found regularly and without exception in every digression and prefatory section of which the subject is abuses in

[3] The first to draw attention to Swift's use of this particular method in *A Tale of a Tub* and elsewhere was Ricardo Quintana in "Situational Satire: A Commentary on the Method of Swift," *University of Toronto Quarterly*, XVII (1948), 130–36. In more recent years, this technique has been the subject of an entire book (William B. Ewald, Jr., *The Masks of Jonathan Swift* [Oxford, 1954]) and has formed a part of every discussion of Swift's satirical methods.

learning. They are just as consistently absent, whether alone or in combination, in every one of the sections devoted to abuses in religion, including Section IX, the "Digression concerning Madness." In the absence of this impersonation, we are certainly justified in regarding the "speaker" in the sections concerned with abuses in religion as Swift himself, sometimes adopting the irony of pretended impartiality, at other times employing the inverted irony of pretended praise, but at no time assuming the identity of another person. There are, it is true, a few paragraphs in this portion of the *Tale*, never more than two in any section, which interrupt the progress of the narrative (or, once, of the description of madness) in order to glance at the moderns, and here, in perfect consistency with the momentary change of subject, the impersonation is revived.[4] But it is just because the momentary impersonation is so unexpected and so out of keeping with the remainder of the section in which it appears that, quite apart from the abrupt and unexplained shift of subject, these paragraphs bear the mark of being later insertions. In fact, Swift himself bore testimony to these later additions when he remarked in the "Apology" that he had inserted "one or two remarks" in reference to the ancients-moderns controversy into the "body of the book," by which term he several times refers to the satire on abuses in religion. Their presence simply reminds us, although this was not Swift's purpose, of the enormous difference in manner between the two satires.

A Tale of a Tub, then, is a satire which deals with two separate subjects, in two separate groups of sections, by means of two separate satirical methods. In addition, the two parts of the book were written at two separate periods of time.

The portion of the *Tale* which deals with abuses in learning can be dated with a fair degree of accuracy, for several of the prefatory sections carry dates in the text itself, while Swift added notes to several others in the first and fifth editions of the book which specify the dates for these sections as well. Finally, Guthkelch and Nichol Smith have been able to date additional sections from internal evidence.[5] According to this evidence, the sections of

---

[4] These additions consist of two paragraphs in Section IV (I, 65–66, 70), one in Section VI (p. 86), and one in Section IX (p. 106), as well as parts of two other paragraphs, one of which is in Section VI (p. 84), the other in Section XI (pp. 130–31).

[5] See A. C. Guthkelch and David Nichol Smith (eds.), *A Tale of a Tub . . . by Jonathan Swift* (2nd ed., Oxford, 1958), pp. xliii–xlvii.

A Tale of a Tub which pertain to abuses in learning were written after June, 1697, and probably occupied Swift from the summer of that year until about the time of Sir William Temple's death in 1699, if not longer. That is to say, they were written during the latter part of Swift's third and final residence with his patron, which had begun in May, 1696. The text of "The Preface" is dated August, 1697, the text of the "Dedication to Prince Posterity" is dated December, 1697, and the same year is assigned to "The Introduction" by one of Swift's notes to the first edition, and to "The Conclusion" by one of his notes to the fifth edition. None of the sections pertaining to abuses in learning, furthermore, is likely to have been written before June, 1697, for they all contain references to Richard Bentley, whose first contribution to the ancients-moderns controversy appeared at that time. It is not unlikely, however, that Swift was still adding to this portion of his book in 1698 and 1699.

The portion of *A Tale of a Tub* which satirizes abuses in religion was written somewhat earlier than that which deals with abuses in learning. According to the available evidence, Swift wrote his religious satire in 1695 and 1696, that is to say, during the time that he held the prebend of Kilroot. For the date at which he finished writing the religious sections we have Swift's own testimony, given in such precise terms that it has been accepted by all modern commentators on *A Tale of a Tub*. In the "Apology" he declares that "the greatest Part of that Book was finished above thirteen Years since, 1696, which is eight Years before it was published" (I, 1). In his effort to specify the date exactly, he gives it in three different forms: "1696," "eight years before it was published" in 1704, and "above thirteen years since." Now, although the fifth edition did not appear until 1710, the "Apology" itself is dated June 3, 1709, so that the year 1696 is again confirmed as the time at which the religious satire was finished.

Swift's selection of the term "finished," however, implies that he had begun the composition of this portion of his book before 1696. The problem is to determine how long before that date Swift commenced writing his religious satire. The most recent detailed examination of this problem was offered by Herbert Davis in the introduction to his edition of *A Tale of a Tub*. Mr. Davis argues that it is most unlikely that Swift began writing his satire before 1695. During the period of his second residence with Temple, from 1691 until 1694, Swift was almost wholly preoccupied, as Mr. Davis shows, with his early efforts in verse, to the probable exclusion of any other literary activities. At the time of this second residence, Mr. Davis points out,

> there is no word in any of the few available letters to suggest that he had by him even the rudiments of a satire in prose; and it is difficult to believe that if *A Tale of a Tub* had been begun or even thought of so early as this, and before Swift had taken orders, he would not have mentioned it in the *Apology*, when he was defending it as a youthful work.[6]

Mr. Davis proceeds to offer a convincing argument for Swift's having begun writing his religious satire in 1695 when, following his ordination, he became prebendary of Kilroot, where he remained until his return to Temple in May, 1696. Presumably, Swift left Kilroot with this portion of his book finished or nearing completion. Leisure he must have had in plenty in his remote country cure; as Mr. Davis remarks, "there was only one thing for an ambitious man to do there, and that was to write."[7]

Corroborative evidence in support of Mr. Davis's argument is supplied, as it happens, by Swift's own testimony. In a note on Section II which he added to the fifth edition, Swift writes: "*This shews the Time the Author writ, it being about fourteen Years since those two Persons were reckoned the fine Gentlemen of the Town*" (I, 52). Now Swift almost certainly wrote the notes for the fifth edition at about the same time that he wrote the "Apology" (the summer of 1709), for he refers to them as already written or in the course of being written at the end of the "Apology" itself. Section II, furthermore, to which the note refers, contains the beginning of the tale of the three brothers and therefore, presumably, the earliest portion of the narrative to be written. A date fourteen years before 1709 gives us, consequently, 1695 as the year in which Swift began writing his religious satire, unless his memory was seriously at fault. But if, along with all modern commentators on *A Tale of a Tub*, we accept as reliable Swift's memory in 1709 of the date at which he finished his religious satire, we ought to be willing to accept with equal assurance his recollection, also

[6] *Prose Works*, I, xiv.
[7] *Ibid.*, I, xv.

8

in 1709, of the date at which he began this portion of his book. If Swift began writing his religious satire in the year in which he took up residence at Kilroot, and finished it in the year in which he took leave of his parish, it is certainly the most reasonable course to assume that it was at Kilroot that he wrote most if not all of the religious sections of *A Tale of a Tub*.

Swift finished writing his first satire, then, approximately a year before he began writing his second. In the light of this evidence, Guthkelch and Nichol Smith were fully justified in stating that "the addition of the 'abuses in Learning' to the 'abuses in Religion' was an afterthought." [8] Swift's statement that his religious satire was "finished" in 1696 implies that it was substantially in this same form that it ultimately appeared in 1704. But it does not imply that he did not revise or even add to a manuscript which he waited eight years to publish. Although they are relatively few in number, certain additions to the text of the religious satire can be detected which are in every case explainable by the afterthought of combining a second satire with that already written. I drew attention earlier to Swift's statement that he inserted "one or two remarks" in reference to the ancients-moderns controversy into his religious satire. These paragraphs could scarcely have been added earlier than 1697 in view of their subject and the method of impersonation used, and in fact the only internal evidence offered by any of these paragraphs points to a date after September, 1697.[9] The purpose of these additions, slight though they were, seems to have been to provide a few mechanical links between the two portions of *A Tale of a Tub* and thus to serve the same function in the sections devoted to abuses in religion as was performed by the inclusion of the pulpit among the three wooden machines described in "The Introduction," which is otherwise concerned exclusively with abuses in learning. Again, it is not unlikely that the concluding portion of Section IX, which is devoted to finding employment for the inhabitants of Bedlam and is not a part of the religious satire at all, was added at a date after

[8] *A Tale of a Tub*, p. xlvi.

[9] See the allusion in the concluding paragraph of Section XI to Sir Humphrey Edwin, who was elected Lord Mayor of London in September, 1697. I suspect, although on no better grounds than the style, that the first two paragraphs of this section may also have been added later.

the rest of the section was finished.[10] Finally, although the religious satire of the *Tale* itself was finished in 1696, Swift wrote and published along with the *Tale* a "fragment" of religious satire, *The Mechanical Operation of the Spirit*, which belongs to a later period, when he was writing or had even finished his satire on abuses in learning. For not only is this separate attack on Puritan enthusiasm conveyed through the impersonation of a modern author, but internal evidence indicates that it was written no earlier than September, 1697.[11] If there were other additions besides these, they were made so skilfully as to prevent detection.

Differing so markedly in subject, method, and circumstances of composition, the two satires of *A Tale of a Tub* reveal an equally significant difference in their immediate backgrounds. Both of these backgrounds consisted of controversies in which Swift took more than a passing interest. Each offered him, at his first venture into prose satire, targets for ridicule, and even materials for parody, in the writings of those disputants whom he chose to attack. Swift drew attention to this fact himself when he pointed out that some passages in his book "are what they call Parodies, where the Author personates the Style and Manner of other Writers, whom he has a mind to expose" (I, 3). But it was not only the side he disliked in these controversies which provided Swift with materials for his satire. He was also indebted to the side he favored, although for materials of a different kind. Here it was the assumptions and attitudes of those who shared Swift's dislike for certain groups, and the methods they had already employed elsewhere for attacking the same targets, that provided him with elements of thought and conventions of treatment which he could use, often in new and different ways, when he came to contribute to these disputes himself by means of a prose satire.

The immediate background of Swift's satire on abuses in learning, as he pointed out in the "Apology," is to be found in two separate but closely related disputes: the quarrel of William Wotton with Swift's patron and the Phalaris controversy, both of which engaged a great many combatants besides Swift during the fifteen

[10] This final portion (I, 110–14) not only ignores the abuses in religion with which the rest of Section IX is concerned but arbitrarily introduces the impersonation of the modern author.

[11] Again the evidence is provided by an allusion to Sir Humphrey Edwin (I, 182).

years between 1690 and 1705.[12] Swift's participation in this ancients-moderns controversy was practically insured by his connection with Temple, and in his own contribution he drew freely
upon the previous contributions to both sides of the quarrel, as
several valuable studies of the background of this satire have
shown.[13]

The young man who was the friend and companion of Sir
William Temple at the time he wrote his satire on abuses in learning was a newly ordained clergyman residing in his first parish
when he wrote his satire on abuses in religion. The background
of this religious satire was a controversy which lasted much longer
than fifteen years and engaged far more than a dozen or so
disputants, but it was as intense in its own way as was the ancients-moderns controversy. It consisted of a number of disputes
concerning religion in which apologists of the Church of England
were engaged with various opponents. In entering this controversy, Swift made less use of the writings of those combatants
whom he had "a mind to expose" than he was to do when he
came to write his second satire. But his debt to the other side,
the apologists for the Church of England, was, if anything,
greater.

His purpose in his religious satire, Swift explained in the
"Apology," was to expose "the Follies of Fanaticism and Superstition." In the service of this intention, his satire "raillies nothing
but what [the Anglican clergy] preach against. . . . It Celebrates
the Church of *England* as the most perfect of all others in Discipline and Doctrine, it advances no Opinion they reject, nor condemns any they receive" (I, 2). Farther on he remarks that "it will
be obvious to every Reader, that . . . the Abuses he notes [are]

[12] Some twenty-one contributions to the two disputes, in addition to
A Tale of a Tub and *The Battle of the Books*, appeared during this
time and were the work of at least sixteen writers.

[13] See especially R. F. Jones, "The Background of the *Battle of the
Books*," *Washington University Studies*, VII (1920), 99–162; Emile
Pons, *Swift: les années de jeunesse et le "Conte du tonneau"* (Strasbourg and London, 1925); R. F. Jones, *Ancients and Moderns: A
Study of the Background of the Battle of the Books* (St. Louis, Mo.,
1936); Miriam K. Starkman, *Swift's Satire on Learning in "A Tale of
a Tub"* (Princeton, N. J., 1950). Professor Jones and Mrs. Starkman
have also related this background to other ancients-moderns controversies earlier in the seventeenth century.

such as all Church of *England* Men agree in, nor was it proper for his Subject to meddle with other Points, than such as have been perpetually controverted since the Reformation" (I, 4).

If these remarks place rather more emphasis upon a panegyric of the Church of England and less upon an attack on its enemies than Swift's satire would seem to warrant, this is because he was concerned primarily with answering the charges of impiety which Wotton and William King had leveled against the book. The sincerity of his remarks is not likely to be questioned today.[14] In respect to the background of his religious satire, however, the emphasis which Swift gives to the apologists of his own church is perfectly just. He could speak with some authority of what it was that the Anglican clergy preached against, of what opinions they vociferously rejected, and which opinions they agreed on and defended in their sermons and discourses. "The Author was then young, his Invention at the Height, and his Reading fresh in his Head," Swift tells us in the "Apology" (I, 1). That some of this reading had been in the religious polemics of various Anglican apologists is evident from the contributions he levied upon them in his satire on abuses in religion.

All "Church of England men" were agreed as to what these abuses were. But the apologists of that church by no means all agreed in their ways of attacking them. They differed in their assumptions about their opponents, in their use of various rhetorical conventions for attacking them, and even in some of the religious attitudes reflected in their polemics. It is these differences which distinguish clearly discernible groups among the Anglican apologists of Swift's own day. To one of these groups I have given the name of "Anglican rationalists" in this study, and in the chapters which follow I shall offer evidence to show that it was to this group in particular that Swift was indebted for many of the materials in his religious satire.

[14] The general acceptance of Swift's religious orthodoxy dates from the appearance of Ricardo Quintana's *The Mind and Art of Jonathan Swift* (New York, 1936), although it had been recognized by a few earlier writers, such as F. M. Darnall, in "Swift's Religion," *Journal of English and Germanic Philology*, XXX (1931), 379–82. Several studies of Swift's religion, particularly in relation to his sermons, have been published in more recent years by Louis A. Landa. See especially his valuable introduction to Swift's sermons in *Prose Works*, IX, 97–137.

Chapter 2

REASON AND REVELATION

The satire on abuses in religion in *A Tale of a Tub* is first introduced and most easily understood in the tale of the three brothers, in which Swift satirizes "fanaticism and superstition" as they appear to him under the guise of Puritanism and Catholicism. Swift himself referred to this tale as an "allegory," and it is by this name that it has usually been described. In calling his tale an "allegory," he meant to indicate that it is a story with symbolic counterparts beyond the fiction itself. It is not an allegory, however, in the strict sense, that is, a didactic piece of fiction, such as *Pilgrim's Progress*, which offers personified forms of general qualities from which the reader is expected to draw deductive proof of some argument by particularizing to his own situation. Instead, the tale of the three brothers is a parable, and, like all parables, it presents specific characters engaged in a particular action in such a way that by providing a simple equation for each of the characters and objects in the apologue the reader can infer a parallel argument. Normally, the values for which the characters and objects stand in a parable remain constant throughout. This is only partially true of Swift's parable. Because he is epitomizing the entire history of Christianity in the simple account of the three brothers, the individuals or groups for which the brothers themselves stand undergo several shifts in the course of the story. Although the symbolic equivalent of the characters alters from time to time, however, that of the action itself and of such objects as the will and the coats remains constant throughout the story. And these sym bolic equivalents are identified by Swift himself in the notes to his book wherever the meaning itself is not sufficiently obvious.

By concentrating entirely upon the simple equations of Peter for Catholicism and Jack for Puritanism in the latter part of the tale, most commentators have allowed the dramatic possibilities of these two equations to overshadow the argument of the parable as a whole. In order to grasp the intent of this parable, it is necessary to distinguish what is essential to Swift's tale of the three brothers from what is merely ornamental. That which is essential to the parable consists of all those incidents which, taken together, provide an argument concerning the history of Christianity and the respective roles in that history which have been played by Catholicism, Puritanism, and Anglicanism. None of these incidents could be subtracted from the story without affecting the essential line of the narrative. Other episodes, on the other hand, are purely ornamental. If any of these were omitted from the tale, the narrative itself and its parallel argument would remain essentially the same. Their purpose is simply to dramatize as many as possible of the "follies" of Catholicism and Puritanism which derive from the roles they play in this history.

The essential story of the three brothers and the parallel argument which it offers concerning the history of Christianity can be briefly summarized as follows. In Section II, which presents the early history of Christianity, we are told that a certain father (Christ) left each of his sons a coat (the Christian religion) as well as a will (Holy Scripture) containing *"full Instructions in every particular concerning the Wearing and Management"* of their coats (I, 44). These instructions "consisted wholly in certain plain, easy Directions" (I, 121) which were equally comprehensible to all of the brothers, who, having been born at the same time, "neither could the Mid-Wife tell certainly which was the Eldest" (I, 44), were directed by their father to live together in perfect equality. Furthermore, on one point the will was particularly firm: "It was the main Precept in it, with the greatest Penalties annexed, not to add to, or diminish from their Coats, one Thread, without a positive Command in the Will" (I, 49). In other words, the doctrines and precepts of Christianity as set forth by Christ, we are told, are contained in Holy Scripture alone, unsupplemented by any other source, and sufficiently plain to be literally and exactly interpreted by the reason of every individual.

For the first seven years (centuries) the three brothers, who at this point in the story are not distinguished by names and represent together the early Christians, follow their father's instructions literally and, since the terms of the will are so simple and clear as to leave no grounds for misinterpretation, live in perfect harmony with one another. At length, however, the three brothers succumb to the charms of the "Dutchess *d'Argent, Madame de Grands Titres,* and the Countess *d'Orgueil*" (covetousness, ambition, and pride). As a result, it now becomes their joint interest to alter the terms of the will so that they can adorn their coats in accordance with changing fashions. In order to accomplish their purpose (the corruption of the Christian religion), two of the brothers place themselves under the authority of the third, who now begins to be distinguished by the name of Peter and comes to stand for the Papacy throughout the remainder of the story, while his brothers at this point in the story represent medieval Christians or, for that matter, the Catholic faithful of any age. Peter manages to find authority for altering the coats to his own and his brothers' satisfaction by two means. One is his distorted interpretation of the will itself, his habit of finding "mysteries" in the plain directions which it contains, and his assumption of the right to explain these mysteries in an authoritative manner. The other is his habit of resorting to oral tradition to supplement the directions laid down in the will, on the basis of the following theory: "*Brothers,* said he, *You are to be informed, that, of Wills,* duo sunt genera, *Nuncupatory and scriptory.*" Swift's own note on this passage reads: "*By this is meant* Tradition, *allowed to have equal Authority with the Scripture, or rather greater*" (I, 51). In other words, the practice of the Papacy in deriving the doctrines of Christianity from both tradition and Scripture and of interpreting these by the teaching authority of the Church has replaced Christ's original command that the beliefs and practices of his religion should be derived from Holy Scripture alone, as interpreted by the reason of every individual.

At length, in Section IV, Peter having locked up the will and begun to pronounce theories ex cathedra which directly contradict common sense, his behavior becomes so outrageous that his two brothers throw off his yoke and turn again to their father's will. That is to say, the two brothers, who at this point begin to be distinguished by the names of Jack and Martin and come to stand for Calvin and Luther, effect a reformation by rejecting tradition and the teaching authority of the Papacy and returning to Scripture as the unique standard of Christian faith.

In Section VI, Martin and Jack set about the task of carrying out their father's injunctions, as revealed by the will, and of removing the ornaments which have been added to their coats. In other words, the reformers set about recovering the pure religion of early Christianity by getting rid of the accretions which have been added to the fabric of religion. At this point the symbolic equivalent for the two brothers undergoes its fourth and final change. Jack and Martin no longer stand for Calvin and Luther as the historical leaders of the Reformation but for the Puritans and Anglicans, respectively. This shift in the roles of Jack and Martin is perfectly appropriate, not only because of the Calvinist antecedents of the Puritans, but because in Swift's view Luther was the father of the English Reformation.[1]

Although united in a common purpose — that of restoring their coats in accordance with the directions in their father's will — the two brothers go about their task in quite different ways. That is to say, assuming the same unique standard of faith — Holy Scripture — the Puritans and the Anglicans apply to the interpretation of its tenets altogether different methods. Martin brings reason and moderation to the task of fulfilling his father's directions and restoring his coat to its original simplicity. Jack, on the other hand, proceeds with such fervor that he only succeeds in tearing and bedraggling his coat until, angered by the result and by Martin's attempts to reason with him, he runs mad from spite and vexation. Two speeches, indicative of the spirit and method of the two brothers, are contrasted. That by Martin is a reasonable exhortation

[1] See Swift's remark in *A Preface to the . . . Bishop of Sarum's Introduction*: "The Reformation owed nothing to the good Intentions of King *Henry*: He was only an Instrument of it, (as the Logicians speak) by Accident; nor doth he appear throughout his whole Reign, to have had any other Views, than those of gratifying his insatiable Love of Power, Cruelty, Oppression, and other irregular Appetites. But this Kingdom, as well as many other Parts of *Europe*, was at that Time generally weary of the Corruptions and Impositions of the *Roman* Court and Church; and disposed to receive those Doctrines, which *Luther* and his Followers had universally spread" (*The Prose Works of Jonathan Swift*, ed. Herbert Davis [Oxford, 1939 —] IV, 73).

to moderation and a plea for resolving differences in a spirit of charity (I, 87). The other and longer speech by Jack is a ferocious diatribe against eyes, which he denounces as "*blind Guides*" and "*foolish Lights, which conduct Men thro' Dirt and Darkness, till they fall into a deep Pit, or a noisom Bog*" (I, 123–24). Jack is speaking here, literally, of the eyes of the body and defending his own habit of going about with his eyes shut. Reason, however, was often spoken of as the eye of the soul, and his speech is clearly a parody of the sectarian diatribes against "carnal reason."

The contrasting spirit behind these two speeches is reflected in the wholly different behavior of the brothers. For Martin is intent upon preserving the fabric of his coat in the course of restoring it to its original condition, and he therefore applies to the directions in his father's will the most reasonable interpretation consistent with his goal. Where he can remove Peter's ornaments without damaging the fabric, he follows the literal directions in the will. But where this is not possible, his reason suggests the best course for meeting eventualities not provided for by his father's literal directions.

> For the rest, where he observed the Embroidery to be workt so close, as not to be got away without damaging the Cloth, or where it served to hide or strengthen any Flaw in the Body of the Coat, contracted by the perpetual tampering of Workmen upon it; he concluded the wisest Course was to let it remain, resolving in no Case whatsoever, that the Substance of the Stuff should suffer Injury; which he thought the best Method for serving the true Intent and Meaning of his Father's *Will* [I, 85].

Jack, on the other hand, acts from a "quite different Spirit." Far from being guided by reason, he follows a humor which he honors "with the Title of *Zeal*." Guided by this fervent humor, he first succeeds in reducing his coat to tatters and then runs mad. And in all his later behavior, as in his manner of removing the ornaments from his coat, his sole aim is to act only according to the literal directions in the will. "He resolved to make use of it in the most necessary, as well as the most paltry Occasions of Life. . . . not daring to let slip a Syllable without Authority from thence" (I, 122). In other words, the parable suggests that Anglicanism has reformed the Christian religion almost to its original purity by interpreting Scripture according to reason, while Puritanism, by its abandonment of reason and its fanatical literalism toward Scripture, has succeeded in producing what is only a parody of Christianity.

The essential subject of Swift's narrative, then, is the problem of how to interpret the father's will in reference to the wearing and adornment of the coats he has left his sons and the various ways in which this problem is met by each of the three sons. The parallel argument offered by Swift's parable is that the crucial turning points in the history of Christianity, accounting for its primitive purity, its various corruptions, and its genuine reformation, have resulted from the different answers, provided by various groups, to the question of what the standard of Christian belief and worship is and how this standard is to be interpreted by Christians.

In addition to the essential line of action which I have just summarized, Swift catalogues at appropriate points in his story a number of ridiculous antics in which Peter and later Jack engage. This permits him to ridicule a number of specific doctrines and practices of Catholicism (such as auricular confession, purgatory, and transubstantiation), or of Puritanism (such as predestination, interminable prayers, and opposition to vestments). Whatever the specific targets of these ornamental episodes, however, Peter is always portrayed as a mountebank and bully, while Jack is pictured as a madman.

There is nothing, at first sight, to distinguish Swift's treatment of Catholic and Puritan beliefs and practices in most of these ornamental episodes, when taken by themselves, from the broad tradition of abuse common to practically all Anglican polemics against their religious opponents at this time, except for the heightened comedy provided by the dramatic possibilities of his narrative. But the argument of the parable itself is by no means so common to Anglican religious polemics as a whole. Comparison of Swift's parable with that in John Sharp's sermon which has often been suggested as the source for the tale of the three brothers reveals how different Swift's argument is from the more usual one.[2] Sharp's parable relates how a certain father bequeathed a large estate to his children which they and their descendants were to

[2] Sharp's parable is reprinted in its entirety by Guthkelch and Nichol Smith (eds.), *A Tale of a Tub . . . by Jonathan Swift* (2d ed.; Oxford, 1958) pp. xxxii–xxxiv.

share in perfect equality. In time, however, one of the descendants usurped the entire estate for himself and dispossessed the other heirs. When they protested, appealing to the father's will for their right to share in the estate, the usurper replied, with a logic all his own, that his recent seizure of the estate had never been protested by earlier generations of the family and therefore his title to the estate was secure. The parable ends with the disinherited cousins protesting against this logic and appealing again to their rights under the will.

The argument of Sharp's parable is obviously quite different from Swift's. It is designed to answer the argument "That if we cannot shew a visible church distinct from the Roman, that hath in all times, from the beginning, oppos'd the doctrines and practices of the present church of Rome, then it will undeniably follow, that the present church of Rome is the only visible church." [3] Quite apart from the fact that Puritanism does not figure in the parable, Sharp's choice of an estate (representing the visible church) as the father's bequest instead of the coats (representing the Christian religion) of Swift's parable, and his use of the will as a legal document giving rights of ownership to this estate (i.e., equal authority in the visible church for the various national "churches") instead of as a list of directions governing the wearing and management of the coats (i.e., the beliefs and practices of the Christian religion), points to the totally different argument which he offers concerning the history of Christianity. For Sharp the differences between the Church of England and the Catholic Church turn upon the question of whether the different national "churches" share equal authority or are subject to the See of Rome. For Swift, on the other hand, these differences and those with Puritanism all turn upon the question of the proper standard of Christian belief and practice and the correct method of interpreting this standard.

Sharp's view of the question was by no means unusual. It is one of the most common themes of Anglican apologetics. Four years before Sharp preached his sermon, Dryden gave expression to the idea in *Religio Laici* (1682), including all the essentials, even to the mention of the will and the estate (ll. 388–97). Swift's view of the question was by no means so common. It was the "trademark" of a minority group of highly articulate Anglican divines

[3] *Ibid.*, p. xxxii.

who made it the cornerstone of their apologetics in dealing with Catholicism and Puritanism. This is the group which I shall refer to in this study as the "Anglican rationalists."

The Anglican divines who composed this group are usually referred to by several other collective terms. They include, in the first place, certain figures such as Henry More, Ralph Cudworth, George Rust, and Henry Hallywell, who are known to history as the "Cambridge Platonists." They include also certain other divines such as Edward Stillingfleet and John Tillotson, who are usually referred to as the "Latitudinarians." Finally, they include as well still other writers such as Joseph Glanvill who were in many respects independent of these two famous groups. The collective terms by which some of these divines are more commonly described serve to emphasize either the important contribution which several of them made to a philosophical movement in the seventeenth century or the major role played by several others in the movement toward toleration in English history. In choosing the name "Anglican rationalists" as a collective term for all of them, I wish to emphasize a characteristic they shared, in spite of their other differences. This is the characteristic which distinguishes them as apologists of the Church of England from other contemporary apologists of that church in the common defense against Puritan and Catholic antagonists. And what was specifically characteristic of their apologetics was a theory about the role of reason in the discovery and practice of the doctrines of the Christian religion which they employed as their principal weapon against Puritans and Catholics alike.

The popular conception of this group is such as to make the Anglican rationalists appear a most unlikely influence upon Swift's religious attitude as this is usually interpreted. On the one hand, the divines whom I have named are described as "unorthodox" Christians who paved the way for eighteenth-century deism by teaching that "whether you looked without or within, Nature (without any supernatural revelation) offered you all that was needful for salvation." [4] On the other hand, as the older view of Swift as a skeptic in religion has disappeared, it has given place to

[4] Basil Willey, *The Eighteenth Century Background* (London, 1950), p. 8 (see especially pp. 3–14). But also see the answer to this view by S. L. Bethell, *The Cultural Revolution of the Seventeenth Century* (London, 1951), chap. ii.

a view of him as a fideist in the tradition of *Religio Laici*. He is now pictured as a highly conservative clergyman who, as Kathleen Williams recently described him, "saw reason as a potential threat to faith," and for whom the rational religion of the Cambridge Platonists and their allies "must have seemed, like that of their admirer Shaftesbury, too closely allied to the insidious menace of Deism to be acceptable." [5] It is ironical, in fact, that the commentator who was responsible for establishing Swift's undeniable orthodoxy once and for all, Professor Quintana, has been practically alone in continuing to suggest that "in religion he embraced a rational faith" and that this is one of the specific senses in which he can be described as a "rationalist." [6]

The popular conception of Swift and the Anglican rationalists which sees an opposition between their religious views depends upon a false dichotomy between "orthodoxy" and "rationalism" which misinterprets the religious situation in Restoration England. It is a dichotomy which sets up two mutually exclusive groups among Englishmen of that age: the "orthodox," who in accepting the mysteries of the Christian religion were forced to reject reason, and the "rationalists," who in their emphasis upon a reasonable religion necessarily questioned or weakened the orthodox belief in mysteries. A division of this kind assumes that reason and supernatural religion are incompatible. Now while this assumption was shared by the deists and fideists of Swift's day, it was as vigorously denied by others, including Swift himself.

On this crucial question of the role of reason in religion, there are three major attitudes; and in the seventeenth century, as in nearly every other age in the history of Christianity, all three attitudes found expression. Each of them reflects a wholly different assumption as to the grounds of religion itself. One extreme among Englishmen of the time was represented by the deists, who held that reason by itself provides all the necessary grounds for religion, without the need to resort to revelation at all. This atti-

[5] *Jonathan Swift and the Age of Compromise* (Lawrence, Kan., 1958), pp. 30, 34. (See especially chaps. ii and iii, which contain the fullest expression yet offered of the view that Swift was a "modified sceptic" or fideist.) See also Ernest Tuveson, "Swift and the World Makers," *Journal of the History of Ideas,* XI (1950), 54–74.

[6] *Swift: An Introduction* (London, 1955), p. 38. (See especially pp. 33–38.)

tude, alone among the three, is "unorthodox," since, on the premise that reason suffices for discovering all the truths of religion, it excludes mysteries and the other articles of Christian belief which depend upon revelation alone. Deism as one of the important forces in English religious thought, and as one of the major sources of religious controversy, did not become prominent until the 1690's. It had been in existence for some time before this, however, and was attacked from time to time throughout the Restoration period by Anglican rationalists as well as by other divines.[7]

The other extreme was represented by the fideists, who, while opposed to the deists in every other respect, shared with them the same premise as to the incompatibility of reason with supernatural religion. From this common premise, however, they drew a conclusion that was just the opposite of that drawn by the deists, for they insisted that revelation alone can provide the grounds for religion and that reason ceases where religion begins. Thus, all religion has been revealed and there is no such thing as "natural religion." The most famous expression of this attitude at the time, of course, is in *Religio Laici*, where Dryden declares:

> And as those nightly Tapers disappear
> When Day's bright Lord ascends our Hemisphere;
> So pale grows *Reason* at *Religions* sight:
> So *dyes*, and so *dissolves* in *Supernatural Light* [ll. 8–11].

Dryden was not the only fideist among Anglicans. They gave voice to their view of the exclusive role of revelation in religion, not only in print, but much more often in the pulpit, if we are to believe the complaints of the Anglican rationalists against their fellow clergymen.[8] But fideism was particularly associated with

[7] See, for example, Edward Stillingfleet, *A Letter to a Deist* (London, 1677).

[8] See, for example, Joseph Glanvill's complaint against "the dangerous rashness of those inconsiderate Men, who having heard others defame Reason as an Enemy to Faith, set up the same Cry, and fill'd their Oratories with the terrible noise of *Carnal Reason, Vain Philosophy,* and such other misapplyed words of reproach" ("Anti-fanatical Religion, and Free Philosophy," *Essays on Several Important Subjects in Philosophy and Religion* [London, 1676], p. 18). It is clear from the context that the "others" were the Puritans, while the "inconsiderate men" were members of the Anglican clergy. For examples of Anglican fideists, see John Warly, *The Reasoning Apostate, or*

22

Puritanism, especially as represented by the sects, which had long been notorious for their sermons and discourses against "carnal reason," "vain philosophy," and the "wisdom of this world," so far as even to attack the universities themselves as "synagogues of Satan" and "stews of Antichrist." "For *humane learning*," as one of their preachers wrote, "hath it's place and use among *humane things*, but hath *no place* nor *use* in *Christs Kingdome*." [9]

A middle way between these two extremes was pursued by those who adopted the third attitude, which was equally opposed to each of the other two views. These "moderates" maintained that reason and revelation are not incompatible in religion. On the contrary, reason and revelation together provide the grounds for religion, so that each plays its proper role in the religious sphere and neither can be ignored. There were some Puritans, such as Richard Baxter, among the Presbyterians and Congregationalists particularly, who adopted this position but their number was small.[10] Historically, this position represents the mainstream of tradition in the Catholic and Anglican churches. As formulated in the thirteenth century by St. Thomas Aquinas, it is the official position of his church. As reformulated at the end of the sixteenth century by Richard Hooker, it became the position on the grounds of religion of not only the Anglican rationalists but also a great many other members of the Church of England. It was the position, for example, of the "physico-theologians" — those Anglican writers of the Restoration period, such as Samuel Parker, John Wilkins, and John Ray, and of the succeeding era, such as the Boyle lecturers, who confronted atheism with arguments on behalf of natural religion.[11] But as a carefully forged weapon of

Modern Latitude-Man Consider'd (London, 1677), and Thomas Baker, *Reflections upon Learning* (London, 1699).

[9] William Dell, *The Tryal of Spirits* (London, 1653), sig. ee3v. For another typical example, see Samuel How, *The Sufficiencie of the Spirits Teaching without Humane Learning* (London, 1644).

[10] See Richard Baxter, *The Judgment of Non-Conformists of the Interest of Reason in Matters of Religion* (London, 1676). See also Robert Ferguson, *The Interest of Reason in Religion* (London, 1675).

[11] In spite of their common agreement on the subject of the grounds of religion, the physico-theologians differed from the Anglican rationalists in several important respects. In addition to the fact that their exclusive concern as a group in religious polemics was with combating atheism, the physico-theologians also differed from the Anglican rationalists in using very different arguments for natural

religious polemics with which to assail not only atheism but Puritanism and Catholicism as well, the Anglican rationalists of the later seventeenth century made this position peculiarly their own.

In the way in which they shared in common this attitude on the grounds of religion, the Anglican rationalists were of course the heirs of Hooker. But they were also his heirs in the way they made use of this position as their principal weapon against Puritanism, for it was a weapon forged by Hooker himself for use against the Puritans of his own age.

When on behalf of the bishops Hooker wrote his great defense *Of the Laws of Ecclesiastical Polity* (1594) to answer Thomas Cartwright and the other Puritans, the religious situation in Elizabethan England was not unlike that of Martin and Jack after their rupture with Peter. Supporters and opponents of episcopacy were united in their rejection of the authority of the Roman See and in their determination to follow thereafter the authority of Scripture alone in deciding what were the supernatural truths to which they must give assent by faith. Yet the Puritans soon became disaffected with the Establishment for not carrying their reformation far enough. In pulpit and pamphlet they raised a loud clamor against the Church of England "as by law established," not, at first, because of the doctrines to which it required assent, but because its organization, rites, and ceremonies still retained much for which the Puritans found no express warrant in Scripture and which, they charged, owed their introduction to the Roman "Antichrist."

The root of the problem, Hooker perceived, lay in the entirely different views which the supporters of the episcopacy and their Puritan opponents held as to the grounds of religion. In their insistence that the only grounds for religion, and for whatever pertains to religion, such as ecclesiastical rites and ceremonies, are contained in Divine revelation, as expressed in Scripture, the Puritans were ignoring the important part which reason plays in religion as in all other affairs pertaining to men. As a result, Hooker complained:

> the name of the light of nature is made hateful with men; the
> "star of reason and learning," and all other such like helps,

religion, as I shall show in chap. iv. For a recent study of the physico-theologians, see Richard S. Westfall, *Science and Religion in Seventeenth-Century England* (New Haven, Conn., 1958).

beginneth no otherwise to be thought of than if it were an unlucky comet; or as if God had so accursed it, that it should never shine or give light in things concerning our duty any way towards him. . . . A number there are, who think they cannot admire as they ought the power and authority of the word of God, if in things divine they should attribute any force to man's reason.[12]

For the cornerstone of his defense of the Establishment against the Puritans, therefore, Hooker turned to an exposition of the important role which reason shares with revelation in providing the grounds for religion. And for such an exposition, he did not have to develop a new theory. For on the question of the grounds of religion, at least, there was no essential disagreement between Hooker's position and the Catholic position. He relied therefore, to an extent which has only recently been appreciated, upon a re-statement of the Thomistic exposition of the grounds of religion.[13] In the first place, Hooker points out, there are some basic truths of religion which can be discovered by reason alone. These truths, which include the existence and attributes of God, the immortality of the soul, and our paramount duties toward God (Natural Law), constitute natural religion, which is wholly independent of Divine revelation.[14] "Concerning the inability of reason to search out and to judge of things divine," which the Puritans urged in denying natural religion, Hooker replied that "if they be such as those properties of God and those duties of men towards him, which may be conceived by attentive consideration of heaven and

[12] *The Works of That Learned and Judicious Divine, Mr. Richard Hooker* (Oxford, 1890), I, 300 [III, viii, 4]. Because of the many editions of Hooker's works, all references to the *Laws* hereafter will be to Hooker's own division of his work into books, chapters, and sections, as in the reference I have given in brackets here, and will appear in the text.

[13] See Peter Munz, *The Place of Hooker in the History of Thought* (London, 1952), chap. ii and Appendix A. Because Mr. Munz's cross references to the *Summa Theologiae* do not pertain to the matters which I am discussing, I have added cross references of my own below, in order to indicate the extent of Hooker's debt to St. Thomas.

[14] See *Laws,* I, viii (entire chapter). For the parallel Thomistic position on this subject, cf. *Summa,* I, 12, 12 (God's existence and attributes), I, 75, 6 (the immortality of the soul), and I IIae, 94, 3 (Natural Law).

earth; we know that of mere natural men the Apostle testifieth, how they knew both God, and the Law of God" (III, viii, 6).

It was necessary, nevertheless, that God make a revelation to mankind, and this for two reasons. In the first place, reason is not equally strong in all men, so that they could not all have arrived by this means at the truths which natural religion provides. Therefore, God has repeated these natural truths in his revelation, so that what some may know by reason all may know by faith.[15] Secondly, man has a supernatural end, and the duties requisite to be performed by man if he is to attain this supernatural end cannot be known by natural means alone, that is, by reason. For their discovery, a supernatural means was necessary, that is, revelation. As Hooker reasoned:

> All things necessary unto salvation . . . must needs be possible for men to know; and . . . many things are in such sort necessary, the knowledge whereof is by the light of Nature impossible to be attained. Whereupon it followeth that either all flesh is excluded from possibility of salvation, which to think were most barbarous; or else that God hath by supernatural means revealed the way of life so far forth as doth suffice [I, xiv, 3].[16]

Although, therefore, Scripture repeats the truths of religion which some have been able to discover by natural means, its principal intent is "to deliver the laws of duties supernatural" which no man could have discovered by natural means.[17]

But in providing man with this supernatural means, God did not intend that man should no longer make use of the natural means provided by his reason. "When supernatural duties are necessarily exacted, natural are not rejected as needless" (I, xii, 1). The supporters of episcopacy held with the Apostle "that nature hath need of grace"; at the same time, Hooker pointed out, "I hope we are not opposite, by holding that grace hath use of nature" (III, viii, 6). But if they were not opposite to the Apostle in this belief, they were certainly opposite to the Puritans, among whom "an opinion hath spread itself very far in the world, as if the way to be ripe in faith were to be raw in wit and judgment; as if reason

[15] See *Laws*, I, xii (entire chapter). Cf. *Summa*, II IIae, 2, 4.
[16] Cf. *Summa*, II IIae, 2, 3.
[17] See *Laws*, I, xiv, 1.

were an enemy unto religion, childish simplicity the mother of ghostly and divine wisdom" (III, viii, 4). Yet reason is necessary even where religion has been revealed, and it is especially necessary in three respects where the Puritans have dismissed it.

In the first place, reason is necessary to establish the "motives of credibility," or the inducement to assent to Divine revelation. "Scripture teacheth us that saving truth which God hath discovered unto the world by revelation, and it presumeth us taught otherwise that itself is divine and sacred" (III, viii, 13). We are taught otherwise by reason itself, for before we can accept supernatural truths upon God's testimony, we must first of all be assured that there is a God, that his attributes include omniscience and truthfulness, and that he is the author of the Christian revelation. Now reason is responsible for all three of these motives, since the first two are provided by natural religion and the third is a conclusion which reason draws from the proofs (miracles and prophecies) which Christ offered in support of his Divine mission.[18] The Puritans, however, in rejecting reason, must resort to the "testimony of the Spirit," arguing that "if I believe the Gospel, there needeth no reasoning about it to persuade me; if I do not believe, it must be the Spirit of God and not the reason of man that shall convert my heart unto him" (III, viii, 4).

Secondly, reason is necessary for the interpretation of Scripture itself. "Unto the word of God," Hooker writes, "we do not add reason as a supplement of any maim or defect therein, but as a necessary instrument, without which we could not reap by the Scripture's perfection that fruit and benefit which it yieldeth" (III, viii, 10). "The word of God," he adds, "is a twoedged 'sword,' but in the hands of reasonable men." In the hands of the Puritans, it has become an instrument of dissension. Rejecting reason in their interpretation of the Scripture, the Puritans have substituted the "inner light," maintaining "that it is the special illumination of the Holy Ghost, whereby they discern those things in the word, which others reading yet discern them not" ("Preface," iii, 10). But this inner light is not inspiration at all; it is merely "zeal to the cause." Private judgment, Hooker insists, is not a matter of private light and public zeal but the guidance of the individual by reason in two separate senses. Where those things necessary to

[18] See *ibid.*, I, xiv, 1; III, viii, 11–15. Cf. *Summa*, I, 2, 2.

27

salvation are concerned, the individual's own reason is a sufficient guide.

> Some things are so familiar and plain, that truth from falsehood, and good from evil, is most easily discerned in them, even by men of no deep capacity. And of that nature, for the most part, are things absolutely unto all men's salvation necessary, either to be held or denied, either to be done or avoided ["Preface," iii, 2].

In more difficult matters, it is the reason of his teachers which ought to guide the individual's interpretation of Scripture.

> Other things also there are belonging (though in a lower degree of importance) unto the offices of Christian men: which, because they are more obscure, more intricate and hard to be judged of, therefore God hath appointed some to spend their whole time principally in the study of things divine, to the end that in these more doubtful cases their understanding might be a light to direct others ["Preface," iii, 2].

Where reason is applied in this way to the interpretation of Scripture, zeal is needless, dissension impossible.

Finally, there are a great many matters pertaining to religion, particularly as these concern God's church, which are not comprehended in Scripture at all, and here reason as well as the general intent of Scripture must act as guide.

> A number of things there are [Hooker points out] for which the Scripture hath not provided by any law, but left them unto the careful discretion of the Church; we are to search how the Church in these cases may be well directed to make that provision by laws which is most convenient and fit. And what is so in these cases, partly Scripture and partly reason must teach to discern [III, ix, 1].[19]

In rejecting the place of reason in religion, however, the Puritans had made Scripture their only rule, protesting against whatever they found in the Establishment which could not also be found in Scripture. This was the seed, Hooker declared, from which all the dissensions of the Puritans had grown. "For whereas God hath left sundry kinds of laws unto men, and by all those laws the ac-

---

[19] See also the whole of Book II.

tions of men are in some sort directed; they hold that one only law, the Scripture, must be the rule to direct in all things, even so far as to the 'taking up of a rush or straw' " (II, i, 2).

Hence the necessity of Hooker's emphasis upon the role which reason shares with Scripture in all human activities, even where religion is concerned. In summarizing toward the end of his treatise the position from which he assailed the Puritans, he declared:

> The rule to discern when the actions of men are good, when they are such as they ought to be, is more ample and large than the law which God hath set particular down in his holy word; the Scripture is but a part of that rule, as hath been heretofore at large declared. . . . what necessity is there, that every thing which is of God should be set down in holy Scripture? . . . Sufficient it is for the proof of lawfulness in any thing done, if we can shew that God approveth it. And of his approbation the evidence is sufficient, if either himself have by revelation in his word warranted it, or we by some discourse of reason find it good of itself, and unrepugnant unto any of his revealed laws and ordinances [VII, xi, 10].[20]

Hooker's position on the place of reason in religion, as I have summarized it here, became the legacy in two special senses of the Anglican rationalists who followed him. It was, in the first place, a position from which to assail the Puritans of a later age, and as such they naturally availed themselves of it. By upholding reason as an ideal of religious belief and practice, they could denounce or ridicule the Puritan for falling short of this ideal, particularly in three respects: for depending upon the "testimony of the Spirit" instead of upon rational motives of credibility; for resorting to the "inner light" in place of reason for interpreting Scripture; and for making Scripture the only rule of human action, to the exclusion of reason. The role which Swift assigns to Jack in his history of Christianity illustrates two of the three respects in which reason was used by the rationalists as a stick for beating the Puritans. Given the nature of the parable itself, there is no place in it for treating of the motives of credibility. The coats which represent the Christian revelation have been received by the brothers from the hands of their father. Therefore, their genuineness can never be in question. But the contrast between Martin and Jack in Sec-

[20] See also *ibid.*, III, viii (entire chapter).

tion VI turns entirely upon the other two differences: first of all, between Martin's reasonable manner of interpreting his father's will and Jack's dependence upon a furious zeal for the same enterprise and, secondly, between Martin's reliance upon reason for dealing with those eventualities in connection with the condition of his coat which were not covered by directions in the will and Jack's contrasting dependence upon the will alone even in "the most paltry occasions of life." Swift's portrayal of Jack as a madman in the ornamental episodes in Section XI and his picture of Jack as the founder of the sect of the Aeolists in Section VIII, however, depend upon the development by the Anglican rationalists of a rhetorical convention for use against the Puritans which they did not owe to Hooker and which I shall take up in the next chapter.

Hooker's position on the place of reason in religion became the legacy of the Anglican rationalists of the Restoration period in a much broader sense than is indicated by their use of this position for attacking the Puritans. Their continual emphasis upon the importance of reason in religion as a means of defending the Church of England against the Puritans and other antagonists, with whom Hooker had no occasion to deal, became the special characteristic by which the Anglican rationalists were recognized by both friend and foe. Joseph Glanvill, one of the most articulate publicists for the group, wrote an essay in the form of a sequel to Bacon's *New Atlantis* in which he described the aims and principal members of the group. The "Divines of Bensalem," as they are called in his narrative, include both the Cambridge Platonists and the Latitudinarians whom I have named, identified by anagrams upon their real names. In spite of certain philosophical differences among these divines, Glanvill viewed them as united as a group in their common concern "to *demonstrate* the *Truth* and *Reasonableness* of the *Christian Religion*." [21] Another of their

[21] "Anti-fanatical Religion and Free Philosophy," *Essays*, p. 19. Only a part of Glanvill's parable appears in this essay. The rest was never printed. The manuscript of the entire parable, entitled "Bensalem: Being a Description of a Catholick & Free Spirit both in Religion & Learning. In a Continuation of the Story of the Lord Bacon's New Atlantis," is now in the University of Chicago Library. The suppressed portion is partially printed by Jackson I. Cope in " 'The Cupri-Cosmits': Glanvill on Latitudinarian Anti-Enthusiasm," *Huntington Library Quarterly*, XVII (1954), 269–86. Glanvill of

friends, Edward Fowler, bishop of Gloucester, although not a member of the group himself, described their common concern in the same way in a book which he wrote in their defense.[22]

These defenses of the Anglican rationalists and of their common aim were not uncalled for. There were always Anglicans who professed fideism and who distrusted any emphasis upon reason in matters of religion as a wedge by which deism, or, as it was more commonly called during the Restoration period, "Socinianism," might enter the church. It was upon the question of natural religion that these Anglicans took their stand, dismissing it as a myth invented by the deists. As one of their number, Dryden, addressed the deists in *Religio Laici*:

> *Reveal'd Religion* first inform'd thy Sight,
> And *Reason* saw not, till *Faith* sprung the Light.
> Hence all thy *Natural Worship* takes the *Source*:
> 'Tis *Revelation* what thou thinkst *Discourse* [ll. 68–71].

For Anglicans such as these the best course for meeting the threat of deism was, as Glanvill complained, to "defame Reason as an Enemy to Faith," making common cause in this respect at least with the Puritans, as he was not slow to point out: "And *this* they did too at a time when the World was posting a-pace into all kinds of madness; as if they were afraid the half-distracted Religionists [Puritans] would not run fast enough out of their Wits, without their Encouragement and Assistance." [23] Minds such as these could have little sympathy for the Anglican rationalists, whom they viewed as "Reasoning Apostates" who made common cause with the deists and Socinians.[24]

Deism and Socinianism were only minor disturbances before the 1690's, and the Anglican rationalists were neither more nor less

course names other Anglican rationalists, anagrammatically, among the "Divines of Bensalem" besides those who will appear in this study. I have confined my attention to a representative selection of Anglican rationalists who are especially pertinent to a study of the religious background of *A Tale of a Tub*.

[22] See *The Principles and Practices of Certain Moderate Divines of the Church of England (Greatly Misunderstood) Truly Represented and Defended* (London, 1670).

[23] "Anti-fanatical Religion," *Essays*, p. 18.

[24] See the references under n. 8 above, and William Sherlock, *The Danger of Corrupting the Faith by Philosophy* (London, 1697).

distracted by them before this date than were their fellow religionists. When they did address the deists, however, as Stillingfleet did in his *Letter to a Deist*, they made it perfectly clear that they were as opposed to deism as were the Anglican fideists but that, unlike the latter, they felt that the best way to win over the deists was not by denying natural religion but by using it for a bridge over which the deists might be persuaded to come to a belief in supernatural religion. And to a belief in supernatural religion the deist must come if he was fully to embrace religion, for the Anglican rationalists held precisely the same view of the respective ingredients of natural and supernatural religion and their necessary connection with each other as Hooker did. For them, as for Hooker, natural religion, discoverable by reason, included only the existence and attributes of God, the immortality of the soul, and Natural Law.[25] For them too, as for Hooker, supernatural religion had to be revealed in order both to make the truths of natural religion available to all men and to make known new truths which no man's reason could have discovered.[26] Finally, they believed with Hooker that "Nature and Scripture do serve in such full sort, that they both jointly, and not severally either of them, be so complete, that unto everlasting felicity" both are needful.[27]

Swift's adherence to this position is perfectly apparent in his *Letter to a Young Gentleman Lately Entered into Holy Orders*. This is a pamphlet on preaching in which Swift advises the young gentleman to use a plain, unaffected style in his sermons, to try to convince his congregation rather than to move them, and to draw his topics "from *Scripture* and *Reason*." What is particularly relevant here, however, is a long passage in which he deplores the habit of disparaging pagan morality in order to enhance the morality taught by the Christian religion. This habit was common among fideist preachers in both Anglican and Puritan pulpits,

[25] Examples from Tillotson should suffice, since he is most often interpreted as a forerunner of the deists by those who misconstrue the position of the Anglican rationalists. For the constituents of natural religion, see *The Works of Dr. John Tillotson, Late Archbishop of Canterbury* (London, 1820), III, 411–15 (existence and attributes of God); VII, 520–76 and VIII, 1–23 (the immortality of the soul); V, 273–97 (Natural Law).

[26] See *ibid.*, I, 443–65 (Scripture repeats the truths of natural religion); I, 317–89 and III, 409–38 (Scripture reveals new truths necessary to salvation).

[27] *Laws*, I, xiv, 5. See Tillotson, *Works*, V, 298–322.

who used it as a means of attacking the concept of natural religion. The passage deserves extended quotation because of the important light it throws on Swift's view of the grounds of religion.

BEFORE you enter into the common unsufferable Cant, of taking all Occasions to disparage the Heathen *Philosophers*; I hope you will differ from some of your Brethren, by first enquiring what those *Philosophers* can say for themselves. The System of Morality to be gathered out of the Writings, or Sayings of those antient Sages, falls undoubtedly very short of that delivered in the Gospel; and wants, besides, the Divine Sanction which our Saviour gave to his. Whatever is further related by the Evangelists, contains chiefly Matters of Fact, and consequently of Faith; such as the Birth of Christ, his being the Messiah, his Miracles, his Death, Resurrection, and Ascension: None of which can properly come under the Appelation of human Wisdom, being intended only to make us wise unto Salvation. And therefore in this Point, nothing can be justly laid to the Charge of the *Philosophers*; further, than that they were ignorant of certain Facts which happened long after their Death. But I am deceived, if a better Comment could be any where collected upon the moral Part of the Gospel, than from the Writings of those excellent Men. Even that divine Precept of loving our Enemies, is at large insisted on by *Plato*; who puts it, as I remember, into the Mouth of *Socrates*. And as to the Reproach of Heathenism, I doubt they had less of it than the corrupted *Jews*, in whose Time they lived. For it is a gross Piece of Ignorance among us, to conceive, that in those polite and learned Ages, even Persons of any tolerable Education, much less the wisest Philosophers, did acknowledge, or worship any more than one Almighty Power, under several Denominations, to whom they allowed all those Attributes we ascribe to the Divinity: And, as I take it, human Comprehension reacheth no further: Neither did our Saviour think it necessary to explain to us the Nature of God; because I suppose it would be impossible, without bestowing on us other Faculties than we possess at present. But the true Misery of the Heathen World, appears to be what I before mentioned, the Want of a Divine Sanction; without which, the Dictates of the Philosophers failed in the Point of Authority; and consequently the Bulk of Mankind lay, indeed, under a great Load of Ignorance, even in the Article of Morality; but the Philosophers themselves did not. Take the Matter in this Light, and it will afford Field enough for a Divine to enlarge on; by shewing the Advantages which the Christian World hath over the Heathen; and the absolute Necessity of Divine Revelation, to make the Knowledge of the true God, and the Practice of Virtue more universal in the World [IX, 73–74].

Swift's eloquent defense of natural religion is so explicit here as hardly to require comment. It is worth noticing, nevertheless, that Swift specifies two kinds of religious knowledge which not only "the wisest philosophers" but "even persons of any tolerable education" were able to arrive at by the use of reason alone: "the knowledge of the true God" — under which Swift specifies his existence and "those attributes we ascribe to the Divinity" — and "the practice of virtue." But beyond this "human comprehension reacheth no further." Therefore revelation was necessary as a supplement to reason on two scores: first of all, because "the bulk of mankind lay, indeed, under a great load of ignorance" respecting these natural truths until Scripture repeated them in order to make them "more universal in the world," allowing all men to know by faith what some could discern by reason; secondly, because Scripture contains "matters of fact, and consequently of faith," which are not available to "human wisdom" since they concern man's supernatural end, "being intended only to make us wise unto salvation."

The Anglican rationalists, then, as well as Swift, were indebted to Hooker, not only for their principal defense against Puritanism, but for the general view which they shared on the grounds of religion. It was a view which served them equally well in their polemics against the Catholics. But here, because they were engaged with a different antagonist, they showed greater independence from their Elizabethan predecessor. It goes without saying that Hooker was as opposed to the Catholics as were the Anglican rationalists of the Restoration period. But it is important to keep in mind that the climate of Anglican apologetics had altered greatly since Hooker's time.[28] It is significant that Hooker made

[28] For a good recent study of the religious situation as a whole in Restoration England, see G. R. Cragg, *From Puritanism to the Age of Reason* (Cambridge, 1950).

34

his answer to the Puritans his life's work. The Puritans in Hooker's lifetime and long afterward offered a "clear and present danger" to the very existence of the Established Church. As long as this situation continued, as it did for sixty years after Hooker's death, the greatest share of Anglican apologetics was aimed at Puritanism. After 1660, however, with the return of the court from France and the making of the Restoration religious settlement, the whole climate of apologetics changed. Puritanism was still a grievance, but it was no longer a real danger. Simultaneously, however, two other dangers arose, not unconnected with the newly restored court. One of these was atheism, associated in the popular mind with the "Wits" and "Scoffers" who, with Hobbes at their head, were supposed to be influential at court. How great was their number and how real their influence we have no way of knowing. Professed atheists are hard to find in the Restoration period, yet they certainly received a good share of attention from Anglican preachers.

The other danger to the Establishment came from the growing influence of the Catholics at court. Although the official policy toward them remained unchanged after the Restoration, they published books and made converts with greater freedom and success than at any time in over a century. Both of these antagonists had to be faced by Anglican apologists, as indeed they were. For the next thirty years, from about 1660 until 1690, the climate of Anglican apologetics was largely colored by the polemics adopted against these two antagonists, although the Puritans, in the background, were certainly never forgotten. The weapons used against these two antagonists were as various as those which had been employed against the Puritans earlier, but it is understandable that the Anglican rationalists forged theirs from the emphasis upon the place of reason in religion for which they are famous.

Such altogether different antagonists required altogether different approaches, and the most famous polemics of the Anglican rationalists reflect these differences. Nor is it to be expected that they all should have been engaged with the same antagonists. Of Stillingfleet's two greatest books, one, *Origines Sacrae, or A Rational Account of the Grounds of the Christian Faith*, was addressed to the atheists, while the other, *A Rational Account of the Grounds of Protestant Religion*, was addressed to Catholics. Henry More, on the other hand, ignored the Catholics for the most part and won fame as an apologist for his attack on the fanaticism of the Puritans in *Enthusiasmus Triumphatus* and for his answer to the atheists in such books as *An Antidote against Atheism* and *The Immortality of the Soul*. Tillotson, in contrast to More, devoted his only important book, *The Rule of Faith*, to answering the Catholics, with whom he dealt frequently in his sermons as well, but he was noted for the gentleness with which he treated the Puritans. Cudworth, to take one more example, devoted a lifetime to his *True Intellectual System of the Universe*, one of the most ambitious confutations of atheism to appear in any age. Whatever their antagonist, however, the polemics of all these Anglican rationalists were notable for the way in which they made an emphasis upon reason their principal weapon.

In their books addressed to the atheists, of course, reason was the obvious weapon for the Anglican rationalists to use. By concentrating upon the rational arguments for the existence of God and the immortality of the soul, they hoped to win over the atheist to an acceptance of natural religion as a necessary first step toward embracing Christianity. In dealing with the Catholics, however, who of course accepted natural religion as well as revealed religion, their approach had to be entirely different.

In opposing the claims of the Catholic Church, the position of the Anglican rationalists was in some respects the very reverse of their position in opposing the Puritans. For in attacking the Puritans, they took exception to the Puritan view of the grounds of religion, and in this respect, as we have seen, the Anglican rationalists found themselves in agreement with the Catholics. In attacking the Catholics, on the other hand, they objected to the Catholic view of the rule of faith, and here the Anglican rationalists found themselves in complete agreement with the Puritans. The rule of faith is an entirely different question from that of the grounds of religion. It is the question which anyone who accepts supernatural religion, whatever his views on natural religion, must face when he asks where he is to seek that Divine revelation which reason could not discover and to which he gives assent by faith. The Protestant view of the question, common to Anglicans and Puritans alike, was that Scripture alone is the rule of faith.

> A rule of faith [Tillotson wrote] is the measure according to which we judge what matters we are to assent to, as revealed

to us by God, and what not. And more particularly, the rule of Christian faith is the measure, according to which we are to judge what we ought to assent to as the doctrine revealed by Christ to the world, and what not.

And in answer to this question he declared: "The opinion then of the protestants concerning the rule of faith, is this, in general: That those books which we call the Holy Scriptures, are the means whereby the Christian doctrine hath been brought down to us." [29]

The Catholic view of the rule of faith differs from this. According to Catholic teaching, the rule of faith consists in two complementary organs or expressions of the Christian revelation: Scripture and unwritten apostolic tradition. Since the Church is the repository of this tradition as well as the custodian of Scripture, she herself possesses the authority to teach and interpret both to the faithful.[30] The Anglicans rejected the necessity for tradition and with it whatever parts of the Catholic faith found explicit statement only in this tradition. Hooker, in maintaining that the whole of the Christian revelation is contained in Scripture, contrasted as two opposite and equally erroneous extremes the Catholic doctrine that Scripture is not a sufficient rule of faith and the Puritan belief that Scripture is sufficient, not only as a rule of faith, but as the grounds of all religion.[31] And the Anglican rationalists who came after him employed the rule of faith as one of their chief topics for disagreement with the Catholics, alternating attacks upon their antagonists for having "presumed to add so many articles to the Christian religion, upon the counterfeit

[29] *Works*, X, 231, 238–39. See also Henry More, "A Brief Discourse of the True Grounds of the Certainty of Faith in Points of Religion," *Divine Dialogues* (London, 1668), II, 483.

[30] This position is enunciated in a decree of the Council of Trent (Fourth Session, April 8, 1546). For an excellent historical study of the whole question, see George H. Tavard, *Holy Writ or Holy Church* (London, 1959). The decree was variously interpreted by English Catholic apologists of the sixteenth and seventeenth centuries. Tavard points out that "the English Recusants were themselves not of one mind on Scripture and Tradition. Some of them had theological idiosyncrasies of their own" (p. 210). Dryden's exposition of the rule of faith in Part II of *The Hind and the Panther* (1687) exemplifies a common answer to the question offered by English Catholics during the Restoration era.

[31] See *Laws*, II, viii, 5–7. See also I, xiii, 2 and I, xiv, 5.

warrant of tradition, for which there is no ground or warrant from the Scripture" [32] with assertions as to the sufficiency of Scripture as the rule of faith. Perhaps the most elaborate development of this topic for disagreement, both in its assertion of the sufficiency of Scripture and in its attack upon the necessity for tradition, was in Tillotson's classic, *The Rule of Faith*.

Now, in disagreements over the rule of faith, one position is neither more nor less rational than another. Whether it find expression in Scripture alone or in Scripture complemented by tradition, revelation depends upon Divine testimony, not upon the discovery of reason. Yet in contrasting the two different positions on the rule of faith in sermons before their own congregations, though not indeed in treatises addressed to the Catholics themselves, the Anglican rationalists pictured the contrast as one between reason and authority. They were able to do so by emphasizing the manner of interpreting the rule of faith.

Hooker, as we have seen, in stressing the necessity for reason in religion had pointed out that one of its uses was in the interpretation of Scripture. But, in emphasizing the place of reason here, he did so in order to limit the competence of private judgment and to stress the need for public authority. The Puritans, by rejecting human reason and substituting the "inner light," had enlarged the competence of private judgment to the point where any individual, whatever his share of reason, could raise sedition within the church by claiming inspiration for whatever interpretation he might apply to the most difficult parts of Scripture. As a result, Hooker complained,

> it hath already made thousands so headstrong even in gross and palpable errors, that a man whose capacity will scarce serve him to utter five words in sensible manner blusheth not in any doubt concerning matter of Scripture to think his own bare *Yea* as good as the *Nay* of all the wise, grave, and learned judgments that are in the whole world: which insolency must be repressed, or it will be the very bane of Christian religion [II, vii, 6].

By emphasizing the necessity for human reason in interpreting Scripture, therefore, Hooker could insist that controversial pas-

[32] Tillotson, *Works*, V, 15–16.

sages in Scripture be left to those who have the greatest share of reason, while those who have less ought, "when any thing pertinent unto faith and religion is doubted of, the more willingly to incline their minds towards that which the sentence of so grave, wise, and learned in that faculty shall judge most sound" (II, vii, 4). As for "things necessary to all men's salvation," since "they are in Scripture plain and easy to be understood," to the extent that "our children may of themselves by reading understand" (V, xxii, 14), here too there is no need for an "inner light," reason in the sense of mere natural intelligence sufficing.

The Anglican rationalists had experienced sufficient proof of the effects of unrestrained private judgment to have no wish to enlarge the boundaries which Hooker had imposed on it. They continued to caution their congregations that "this liberty of judging, is not so to be understood as to take away the necessity and use of guides and teachers in religion." [33] This being the case, there was no real source of disagreement in the Anglican and Catholic views of how their different rules of faith ought to be interpreted. Anglicans and Catholics both held that the controversial matters of faith should be accepted by the faithful on the authority of their respective churches. For both churches the rational effort expected of those "of the meanest capacity" was simply the natural discernment of the printed word while reading the necessary articles of faith as set down in "plain and easy" terms, whether in Scripture or in the *Douay Catechism*. Their real disagreements over the rule of faith, then, were limited to the rule itself, and in the books addressed to their Catholic antagonists, this was the aspect of the question which the Anglican rationalists preferred to discuss. But, as I have indicated, in their sermons the emphasis was different. Here they stressed the fact that the Catholic position on the rule of faith, by positing a twofold rule of faith which was both written and oral, based the teaching and interpretation of this faith upon the authority of the Church itself, whereas the Protestant view of the rule of faith, by maintaining that the whole of revelation had been set down in Scripture where it could be read by all, interposed no such authority between the individual and the necessary articles of his faith. On this basis, the Anglican rationalists were able to contrast the free exercise of reason per-

[33] *Ibid.*, II, 264.

mitted by their own rule, in that "we allow private persons to judge for themselves in matters of religion,"[34] with an authoritarian denial of this freedom implicit in the Catholic rule of faith. On the one hand, they could express pity for the Catholic faithful as a "poor deluded people" who through fear and intimidation were forbidden the exercise of their own judgment. On the other hand, they could heap abuse upon the Catholic Church itself for suppressing Holy Scripture and forbidding it to the faithful, for adding in the name of tradition numerous accretions to the fabric of religion for which there was no warrant in Scripture, and for demanding a blind and implicit faith in this eclectic body of beliefs, like a "mountebank, who never talks of any thing less than infallible cures."[35]

The role which Swift assigns to Peter in his history of Christianity depends upon this polemical convention developed by the Anglican rationalists. Peter is presented as a clever mountebank and bully who, first, by demanding the right to supplement the clear directions in his father's will by oral tradition and to interpret the "mysteries" in the will on his own authority and, then, by locking up the will altogether is able to add numerous ornaments to the coats and to intimidate his brothers into accepting his outrageous theories. His power over them ceases and they are able to restore their coats only when they have made copies of the will for themselves and demanded the right to judge for themselves how far their coats conform to the directions in the will. Then and only then are they in a position to carry out their father's instructions.

As a means of attacking those parts of the Catholic faith which find explicit statement only in tradition, their theory of the rule of faith and of the rational interpretation of that rule was adequate as far as the Anglican rationalists were concerned. But it obviously was of no help at all in attacking those articles of Catholic faith, such as transubstantiation, which were based upon the interpretation of a scriptural text. Here the Anglican rationalists could not object to the source, which by their own admission was unexceptionable. Instead, they had to devise rational criteria which would enable them not merely to interpret Scripture but to test the articles

[34] *Ibid.*, II, 267.
[35] *Ibid.*, II, 55. For typical examples of such sermons, see II, 37–60; 407–52; 517–41.

of faith derived from it in such a way that they could reject as irrational the Catholic doctrines not accepted by the Church of England. This was an extremely hazardous undertaking, for unless these rational criteria were very carefully formulated, their other antagonists, the atheists, could make use of the same criteria for attacking articles of faith common to Anglicans and Catholics alike, such as the mystery of the Trinity. The theory they developed as to the relation between reason and faith, and the criteria they devised, enabling them to condemn specifically Catholic beliefs as irrational and at the same time to proclaim their own beliefs as rational, reflect quite clearly the perilous course the Anglican rationalists had to pursue between atheistic antagonists on the one side and Catholic antagonists on the other. These criteria were a contribution to Anglican apologetics for which the rationalist divines were in no way indebted to Hooker. They depend, in fact, upon a view of the relation between reason and faith which is altogether different from Hooker's.

In employing against the Puritans the Thomistic view of the relationship between reason and revelation in religion, Hooker depended as well upon the Thomistic conception of two formally distinct orders of knowledge: understanding and belief, or science and faith. Natural religion, since it is arrived at by reason, is a matter of understanding or science. But supernatural religion, which depends upon Divine testimony for its revelation, is a matter of belief, or faith. Each of these, within its own sphere, gives a different kind of certainty: "certainty of evidence," as Hooker calls rational knowledge, and "certainty of adherence," as he calls faith. Rational knowledge is "that which we know either by sense, or by infallible demonstration." The intellect gives assent to knowledge of this kind because it is evident in itself. "The truth of some things is so evident, that no man which heareth them can doubt of them." Therefore, "the mind is constrained to say, this is true." [36] The matters we believe by faith, on the other hand, do not possess their own evidence. The intellect gives assent to knowledge of this kind, not because it is evident in itself, but

[36] The preceding quotations are taken from "A Learned and Comfortable Sermon of the Certainty and Perpetuity of Faith in the Elect," *Works*, II, 587–99. For Hooker's distinction between the orders of reason and faith, see, besides this very important sermon, *Laws*, V, xxii, 5, 8; V, lxiii, 1–2. Cf. *Summa*, II IIae, 1, 4–5.

because we have God's authority for its truth. "Whoso assenteth to the words of eternal life," Hooker writes, "doth it in regard of his *authority* whose words they are" (V, xxii, 8). Although the things that we know by faith are not as evident as the things that we know by reason, nevertheless, Hooker says, their truth is even more certain, since they depend upon the testimony of God, who cannot deceive.

For Hooker, then, the concept of a "rational faith" is impossible. Reason and faith cannot contradict each other, but they complement each other by remaining distinct. It is not to be expected, consequently, that we should be able to understand what we believe, for that which we understand is no longer a matter of faith but of science. Reason was never able to discover the truths of faith, and once revealed they still cannot be properly understood, for they belong to the supernatural order, while the competence of reason is limited to the natural order. "We all know," Hooker writes, "that many things are believed, although they be intricate, obscure, and dark, although they exceed the reach and capacity of our wits, yea although in this world they be no way possible to be understood" (V, xxii, 8). As Hooker views the act of faith, the motives of credibility which are the "preambles of faith" are, as we noticed earlier, rational, but once it has been convinced of the reasonableness of accepting Divine testimony, the intellect assents to the particular articles of that testimony on the impetus of the will.

> The mysteries of our religion are above the reach of our understanding, above discourse of man's reason, above all that any creature can comprehend. Therefore the first thing required of him which standeth for admission into Christ's family is belief. Which belief consisteth not so much in knowledge as in acknowledgment of all things that heavenly wisdom revealeth; the affection of faith is above her reach, her love to Godward above the comprehension which she hath of God [V, lxiii, 1].

Rational criteria, then, such as sense and experience, are helpless to support, much less to test, the things which are of faith. "But the strength of our faith is tried by those things wherein our wits and capacities are not strong" (V, lii, 1). In such trials it is the strength of the Christian's will, supported by Divine grace, that will seal his faith:

> And therefore even then when the evidence which he hath of the truth is so small that it grieveth him to feel his weakness in assenting thereto, yet is there in him such a sure adherence unto that which he doth but faintly and fearfully believe, that his spirit having once truly tasted the heavenly sweetness thereof, all the world is not able quite and clean to remove him from it.[37]

Hooker's dependence upon the Thomistic distinction between the orders of reason and faith was clearly worse than useless to the Anglican rationalists. It was a positive hindrance to their purpose of devising rational criteria for faith whereby they could dismiss transubstantiation and other articles of Catholic belief as irrational. The first thing that was necessary, therefore, was to reject this distinction utterly and to make faith and rational knowledge synonymous. "By *faith*," Stillingfleet wrote to a Catholic adversary, "we understand a rational and discursive act of the mind. For faith being an assent upon evidence, or reason inducing the mind to assent, it must be a rational and discursive act." [38] And Glanvill, expounding and defending the teachings of the Anglican rationalists in his account of the "Divines of Bensalem," emphasized their theory that "*Faith* it self, is an *Act of Reason*." [39]

If faith is an act of reason, then we should be able to understand what we believe. As Bishop Rust assured his readers, "he that can persuade himself that he believes a thing that he does not understand, believes he knows not what." [40] Not only are the articles of faith within the reach of our understanding, but we should be able to test them by the same rational criteria we apply to other kinds of knowledge. These criteria, as developed by More and

[37] "A Learned and Comfortable Sermon," *Works*, II, 589.
[38] *A Rational Account of the Grounds of Protestant Religion* (Oxford, 1844), I, 323.
[39] "Anti-fanatical Religion," *Essays*, p. 17.
[40] *A Discourse of the Use of Reason in Matters of Religion: Shewing, that Christianity Contains Nothing Repugnant to Right Reason; against Enthusiasts and Deists. Written in Latin by the Reverend Dr. Rust, . . . and Translated into English, with Annotations upon It, by Henry Hallywell* (London, 1683), p. 26.

preached by Tillotson, were principally two: the evidence of our senses and the principles of right reason, or natural truths.[41] On the premise that faith must be rational and capable of meeting the test of these criteria, the Anglican rationalists proceeded to denounce the specifically Catholic articles of faith as irrational. In particular they found these criteria useful for attacking the Catholic doctrine of transubstantiation. On the evidence of the senses, they pronounced this an irrational doctrine, since the Eucharist, after the consecration of the Mass, still retains the sensible accidents of bread and wine. "He that can once be brought to contradict or deny his senses," Tillotson writes, "is at an end of certainty; for what can a man be certain of, if he be not certain of what he sees?" Therefore, "every man hath as great evidence, that transubstantiation is false, as he hath that the Christian religion is true."[42]

Their Catholic antagonists objected that were the evidence of the senses to be made the criteria whereby articles of faith were accepted or rejected the mystery of the Trinity would be the next to go. But the Anglican rationalists had foreseen this objection when they formulated these two criteria for testing the reasonableness of any doctrine, and they were ready with an answer. Mysteries are above sense. "There is a wide difference," Tillotson wrote in answer to this objection, "between plain matters of sense, and mysteries concerning God."[43] Since mysteries do not pertain to the senses, it is impossible they should ever contradict them.

On the premise that faith is an act of reason, of course, it was necessary for the Anglican rationalists to do more than simply show that mysteries do not contradict rational criteria. They must show in addition that the articles of their faith, particularly the mysteries, were highly reasonable and capable, in some sense at least, of being understood as other kinds of rational knowledge are. In order to make good this claim against any possible objection from the atheists, they resorted to a distinction between the existence of a thing and the manner of its existence. We can understand the fact or existence of a mystery once it has been re-

[41] See More's "Brief Discourse," *Divine Dialogues*, II, 470–78, and Tillotson's sermon "Of the Trial of Spirits," *Works*, II, 255–81.

[42] "Against Transubstantiation," *Works*, II, 447–48.

[43] For Tillotson's answer to this common objection, see *ibid.*, III, 430–35.

vealed, even though we cannot understand its manner. "In the incarnation of the Son of God," Stillingfleet writes, "the manner of the hypostatical union is to us inevident, but then God doth not require our assent to the manner, but to the truth of the thing itself."[44] Glanvill writes that "the *Immaculate Conception* of our *Saviour*, for instance, is very plain as to the thing, being reveal'd clearly, *That it was*; Though *unexplicable*, and unreveal'd as to the *mode, How*."[45] In order to show that this distinction is not unreasonable, the Anglican rationalists frequently argue from the analogy of natural operations that many of our acts of rational knowledge depend upon a distinction of this kind. Tillotson, defending the reasonableness of the doctrine of the Trinity, writes:

> There are a great many things in nature which we cannot comprehend how they either are, or can be: as the continuity of matter, that is, how the parts of it do hang so fast together, that are many times very hard to be parted: and yet we are sure that it is so, because we see it every day. So likewise how the small seeds of things contain the whole form and nature of the things from which they proceed and into which by degrees they grow; and yet we plainly see this every year.[46]

And Glanvill points out "that we believe innumerable things upon the *evidence* of our *senses*, whose *nature*, and *properties* we do not know. *How the parts of matter cohere*; and *how the soul is united to the body*; are *questions* we cannot *answer*; and yet that such things *are*, we do *not doubt*."[47]

The ornamental episodes in Swift's account of Peter's behavior, portraying various "irrational" doctrines to which he requires his brothers' assent, reflect the convention of Anglican rationalist polemics I have been describing. The long episode in which the doctrine of transubstantiation is satirized, for example, turns on the way in which Peter's outrageous assertion contradicts the evidence of the brothers' own senses and on the way they are finally

[44] *Rational Account*, I, 221.
[45] "Anti-fanatical Religion," *Essays*, p. 29. For other uses of this distinction to show the reasonableness of mysteries, see Tillotson's sermon on the Trinity, *Works*, III, 409–38; Rust, *Discourse of the Use of Reason*, p. 26; Glanvill, *Philosophia Pia* (London, 1671), pp. 176–81.
[46] *Works*, III, 425–26.
[47] *Philosophia Pia*, p. 180.

bullied by Peter into denying this evidence. More than one commentator has found these passages particularly offensive, and much of the evidence for the view formerly expressed by Emile Pons and other critics that Swift was striking at the foundations of Christianity itself has been drawn from these very episodes. Offensive they certainly are by modern standards of religious controversy, but we must remember that they are no more brutal than the invectives of Tillotson and the other Anglican rationalists who denounced these Catholic doctrines to their congregations as "downright impudence." Once we understand the convention of using the evidence of the senses as a criterion for finding these doctrines "irrational," Swift's point of view in ridiculing Peter's dogmas ceases to appear materialistic.

Swift's most articulate expression of this aspect of Anglican rationalist apologetics appears, however, in his sermon "On the Trinity." His purpose here is to expound the doctrine of the Trinity to his unlettered congregation "in such a Manner, that the most Ignorant among you may return home better informed of your Duty in this great Point" (IX, 159), and to convince his listeners that this mystery "can be contrary to no Man's Reason, although the Knowledge of it is hid from him" (IX, 162). He begins his argument for the reasonableness of the mystery of the Trinity by pointing out "that every Man is bound to follow the Rules and Directions of that Measure of Reason which God hath given him; and indeed he cannot do otherwise, if he will be sincere, or act like a Man" (IX, 161). Elsewhere, in his "Thoughts on Religion," Swift had written, "I AM in all opinions to believe according to my own impartial reason; which I am bound to inform and improve, as far as my capacity and opportunities will permit" (IX, 261). "Belief according to reason," Swift assures his congregation, involves testing the articles of belief with such rational criteria as the evidence of the senses, to the extent that "if I should be commanded by an Angel from Heaven to believe it is Midnight at Noon-day; yet I could not believe him" (IX, 161).

The mystery of the Trinity, however, does not contradict these criteria, for it is beyond sense and therefore "this Faith," he concludes, "we may acquire without giving up our Senses, or contradicting our Reason" (IX, 168). In revealing this mystery, "it is plain, that God commandeth us to believe there is a Union and there is a Distinction; but what that Union, or what that Distinction is, all Mankind are equally ignorant, and must continue so, at least till the Day of Judgment, without some new Revelation" (IX, 161). If we distinguish between the fact of the Trinity's existence and the manner of its operation, we can perceive that this article of faith is perfectly reasonable, for we are able to understand the fact, even though we do not understand the manner. "Thus, the whole Doctrine is short and plain, and in itself uncapable of any Controversy; since God himself hath pronounced the Fact, but wholly concealed the Manner" (IX, 167). "And, this is no more than what we do every Day in the Works of Nature, upon the Credit of Men of Learning" (IX, 168). A great many other objects of our rational knowledge depend upon this same distinction between the fact which we understand and the manner which we find incomprehensible. "How little do those who quarrel with Mysteries, know of the commonest Actions of Nature? The Growth of an Animal, of a Plant, or of the smallest Seed, is a Mystery to the wisest among Men." Again, "the Manner whereby the Soul and Body are united, and how they are distinguished, is wholly unaccountable to us" (IX, 164). Yet our reason can comprehend these natural operations, understanding the fact though not the manner, and its knowledge of supernatural matters is of the same essential order.

These, then, were some of the principal ways in which the Anglican rationalists used reason as a weapon of apologetics in opposing the claims of their Puritan and Catholic antagonists.[48] We have seen that their emphasis upon the importance of reason in religion depended upon a conviction which they shared with Hooker as to the place which reason enjoys with faith among the grounds of religion but that they differed from Hooker in attempting to identify reason with faith. It is important to consider whether in going beyond Hooker they had come closer to the deists. We have noticed, of course, an important difference between the Anglican rationalists and the deists in that the former accepted the necessity for supernatural religion in addition to natural religion whereas the latter did not. Yet it is possible that

[48] There were still other ways in which they used reason as a weapon of apologetics, which are not pertinent to Swift. One such way was in their controversy with the Catholics over the "resolution of faith" (motives of credibility). This is described by Louis I. Bredvold in *The Intellectual Milieu of John Dryden* (Ann Arbor, Mich., 1934), 73–129.

in equating reason with faith they had unwittingly undermined the foundations of faith, thus "paving the way for deism," although continuing out of habit and strong conviction to accept suprarational beliefs which were no longer supported by the very principles they professed.

Before we conclude, however, that these divines were formally Christians but really deistic rationalists, we must consider how they found it possible to identify reason with faith and in which direction they extended the boundaries of these two orders of knowledge which for Hooker had been distinct. The rationale behind this identification becomes clear in the series of sermons which Tillotson preached on faith.

> Faith is a persuasion of the mind concerning any thing; concerning the truth of any proposition; concerning the existence, or futurition, or lawfulness, or convenience, or possibility, or goodness, of any thing, or the contrary; or concerning the credit of a person, or the contrary.[49]

Once we accept this definition of faith as a persuasion of the mind concerning anything, it becomes clear that faith in fact comprehends every kind of knowledge, that "faith in this general notion is not opposed to error, and knowledge, and opinion: but comprehends all these under it."[50] If then we consider how we come to be persuaded of anything, we will discover that this persuasion is due to one or the other of several kinds of argument.

> Now all the arguments whereby faith may be wrought in us, that is, a persuasion of any thing, will I think fall under one of these four heads; sense, experience, reason drawn from the thing [demonstrative conclusions], or the authority and testimony of some person.[51]

It only remains then to show that the different kinds of faith are distinguished "according to the variety of objects or things believed." Divine faith is simply a "persuasion of things that concern religion."[52] For some parts of Divine faith we are persuaded "by such reasons as may be drawn from things themselves" (natural

[49] *Works*, IX, 182.
[50] *Ibid.*, IX, 184.
[51] *Ibid.*, IX, 185.
[52] *Ibid.*, IX, 188.

religion), while for other parts we are persuaded by "the testimony or authority of God" (supernatural religion).[53] Quite obviously, More's and Tillotson's method of identifying science and faith is accomplished at the expense not of faith but of science. Faith is a "rational act" only because rational acts have all become acts of faith, and the "infallible demonstration" which Hooker attributed to reason has given place to a mere persuasion that a thing is so.

We can discover further evidence that it is science, not faith, that suffers from the identification of the two by the Anglican rationalists if we notice how Stillingfleet adopts a different tactic for justifying this identification when he addresses another audience: the atheists. Faith, he assures them, is not different in any essential respect from knowledge:

> For the truth of Knowledg depending on this supposition, That there is a GOD, whose goodness will not suffer us to be deceiv'd in the things we clearly understand; there is the same foundation for the act of Faith as for that of Knowledg, *viz.* That GOD will not suffer us to be deceiv'd in matters which himself hath reveal'd to us.[54]

Knowledge, then, quite as much as faith, is a persuasion of the mind the motive for whose credibility depends upon the existence of a God who cannot deceive. On this basis he concludes:

> There is not then any such contrariety between the foundation of Faith and Knowledg, as the Schoolmen have persuaded the World; we see both of them proceed on the same foundation of certainty; all the difference is, Faith fixeth on the veracity of GOD immediately in reference to a Divine Testimony; Knowledg proceeds upon it, supposing no Divine Revelation as to the things it doth discover.[55]

Stillingfleet's premise that the truth of knowledge depends upon the supposition "that there is a God, whose goodness will not suffer

[53] *Ibid.*, IX, 190–209. For More's use of the same comprehensive definition of faith in order to identify science with faith, see his "Brief Discourse," *Divine Dialogues*, II, 467.

[54] *Origines Sacrae, or A Rational Account of the Grounds of the Christian Faith* (7th ed.; Cambridge, 1702), p. 154.

[55] *Ibid.*, p. 155.

us to be deceived in the things we clearly [and distinctly] understand" carries a familiar ring. It is, of course, Descartes' Divine guarantee. But how different is the purpose for which he introduces it! For Descartes the Divine guarantee is the means of restoring on a firmer basis than before the certitude of our clear and distinct perceptions. For Stillingfleet, on the contrary, it becomes the means of weakening the atheist's confidence in such knowledge, to the point where he will admit that it possesses no greater certitude than that of faith and will be obliged to accept the one as well as the other. In this way, faith will gain what rational knowledge has lost.[56]

It should be clear, then, in what sense we can speak of these divines as "rationalists": only in the sense that they employed appeals to reason in the service of their faith. They had perceived that the fideist, in spite of his strong faith, is a philosophical agnostic, since he denies that the existence of God can be demonstrated on rational grounds. In opposing fideism and asserting the claims of natural religion, they were intent on showing that a philosophical certainty of God's existence underlies the claims of supernatural religion. But in the climate of controversy in which they found themselves, with Catholics on one side and atheists on the other, they came to adopt a position in which they did not abandon reason — indeed, they emphasized it more than ever —

[56] Not all Anglican rationalists made use of this particular argument to justify their identification of knowledge with faith. Some realized that Descartes' Divine guarantee could be used to buttress supernatural religion only at the expense of natural religion. Cudworth, for instance, wrote of the Divine guarantee that "though there be a *Plausibility* of *Piety*, in this Doctrine, as making the knowledge of a *God Essentially Good*, so necessary a Precognitum to all other Science, that there can be no *Certainty* of Truth at all without it, yet does that very *Supposition* . . . render it utterly Impossible, ever to arrive at any Certainty concerning the *Existence of a God Essentially Good*; for as much as this cannot be any otherwise proved, then by the use of our *Faculties* of *Understanding, Reason*, and *Discourse*" (*The True Intellectual System of the Universe* [London, 1678], p. 717). Descartes himself never intended that the Divine guarantee, discussed in the fourth, fifth, and sixth of his *Meditations*, should be used to argue that "there is the same foundation for the act of faith as for that of knowledge." On the contrary, he accepted the Thomistic distinction between the two. See Étienne Gilson, *Études sur le rôle de la pensée médiévale dans la formation du système cartésien* (Paris, 1951), pp. 288–90.

but denied it independence to a degree where it was no longer self-supporting and had to rely for its certainty upon faith. Such a position was not new. Historically, this position, which Étienne Gilson has named "theologism," had been embraced by St. Augustine, by St. Anselm, and by numerous other Christian apologists for whom the formula "Credo ut intelligam" expressed the cost at which reason was permitted to remain one of the grounds of religion.[57] Indeed, the reader of Bishop Rust's elaborate attempts to demonstrate the mysteries of the Christian religion is reminded of nothing so much as of the *Proslogion* of St. Anselm.[58]

It has been characteristic of most of the elaborations of this position that they have hardly outlived their designers. So it was with Anglican rationalism. It flourished only as long as the climate of controversy which had called it forth. In the 1690's, the sudden eclipse of Catholicism as a threat to the Establishment was followed almost immediately by the rise to prominence of deism. A new crisis was met by new apologists using a new apologetics. Anglican rationalism rapidly declined into obscurity; for it made no lasting contribution to the church in whose defense it had been devised. When in the last century Anglican thought experienced a resurgence, it was to Hooker that John Keble and Bishop Paget and Dean Church turned once more. The Anglican rationalists, on the contrary, have been remembered only to be misunderstood and to be recast, ironically enough, in the same mold with the deists whom they detested.

[57] See Étienne Gilson, *Reason and Revelation in the Middle Ages* (New York, 1954).
[58] See Rust's *Discourse of the Use of Reason*, pp. 42–46.

Chapter 3

THE REJECTION OF REASON

So far, I have been considering general conventions of Anglican rationalist apologetics which reappear in Swift's parable of the three brothers in *A Tale of a Tub* and in the ornamental episodes connected with Peter's adventures. In turning to a consideration of the ornamental episodes connected with Jack's adventures and of the sects of the tailor-worshippers and Aeolists, we encounter certain rhetorical conventions for attacking the Puritans and the atheists which were the peculiar contribution of some of the Anglican rationalists. It is time, therefore, that we consider the evidence for Swift's acquaintance with specific books by the Anglican rationalists when he came to write the religious satire in *A Tale of a Tub*.

Swift's departure from his parish at Kilroot in May, 1696, to return to Sir William Temple was a hasty one. He left behind his books and other personal effects in the care of the Reverend John Winder, who was to be in charge of the prebend until his return. But Swift did not return, and in January, 1698, he resigned the prebend in favor of Winder. The following April he wrote to his successor asking him to settle his affairs at Kilroot and to send him his books. But Winder moved slowly, and in January, 1699, Swift again wrote him, this time giving him more particular directions for the disposition of his books. Several of them "were not worth the carriage" and were to be thrown out. But several other books which might prove useful to Winder he was to keep as a gift from Swift, adding his friend's name to his own, "and *ex dono* before them in large letters." One of these was *The Works of Edward Reynolds,* bishop of Norwich, whose sermons and treatises are practically free from polemics and could have exerted very little influence on Swift's religious satire. The other was Stillingfleet's *A Rational Account of the Grounds of Protestant Religion,* his principal polemical book against the Catholics. He continues: "The 'Scepsis Scientifica' is not mine, but old Mr. Dobbs's, and I wish it were restored. He has Temple's 'Miscellanea' instead of it, which is a good book, worth your reading. If 'Scepsis Scientifica' comes to me, I will burn it for a fustian piece of abominable curious virtuoso stuff." [1]

We can reasonably assume from his comments of approval or disapproval that Swift had read the four books he mentions either while he was at Kilroot or earlier. Of the three books he recommends to Winder, one was among the foremost Anglican rationalist polemics against the Catholics. To the fourth book which he names, Glanvill's *Scepsis Scientifica,* Swift's reaction was quite different. *Scepsis Scientifica,* which Glanvill published in 1665, is a revised version of his earliest book, *The Vanity of Dogmatizing* (1661). It is an exuberant attack on the "dogmatic" science of the ancients, particularly that of Aristotle, coupled with enthusiastic praise of the modern method of scientific skepticism practiced by the Royal Society, to which the book is dedicated. Such a book, devoted to a contemptuous denigration of the science of the ancients, was not likely to recommend itself to Swift in 1699, and his dismissal of Glanvill's effort as "virtuoso stuff" makes clear that he regarded it as simply one more instance of those boasts on behalf of modern learning which he had recently ridiculed in *The Battle of the Books* and in the portions of *A Tale of a Tub* which he had been at work on since the summer of 1697.[2] There is no evidence that Swift ever read any other book by Glanvill besides *Scepsis Scientifica* or that he was so much as aware of Glanvill's prominent role as an apologist for Anglican rationalism. I shall cite passages from Glanvill's later books from time to time as

[1] *The Correspondence of Jonathan Swift,* ed. F. Elrington Ball (London, 1910), I, 26–30.

[2] This is further borne out, of course, by the fact that Swift couples his contemptuous reference to Glanvill's book with praise of Temple's *Miscellanea.* This book by Swift's patron contains "An Essay upon the Ancient and Modern Learning," which contributed an important share to the background of the satire on abuses in learning in *A Tale of a Tub.*

revealing analogues to the thought of his friend More, but it should be remembered that Glanvill's contributions to Anglican rationalism were probably never "sources" for anything Swift wrote.

The case for Henry More as a possible source of some of Swift's ideas at this time is quite different. There is only one other piece of evidence which directly connects Swift with an Anglican rationalist at the time he was writing his religious satire, and this points unmistakably to More. In a note to one of the frequent mentions of Thomas Vaughan's *Anthroposophia Theomagica* in *A Tale of a Tub,* which he added to the fifth edition, Swift identifies the book as

> *A Treatise written about fifty Years ago, by a* Welsh *Gentle-man of* Cambridge, *his Name, as I remember, was* Vaughan, *as appears by the Answer to it, writ by the Learned Dr.* Henry Moor, *it* [*Anthroposophia Theomagica*] *is a Piece of the most unintelligible Fustian, that, perhaps, was ever publish'd in any Language* [I, 79].

More's answer to Vaughan consists of three parts, published to-gether as a single pamphlet in 1656 under the title of *Enthusiasmus Triumphatus.* These parts are (1) a long preface which bears the same title as the pamphlet itself, (2) "Observations upon *Anthroposophia Theomagica* and *Anima Magica Abscondita,*" and (3) "The Second Lash of Alazonomastix." The preface itself is the most important of all the Anglican rationalist attacks upon the enthusiasm of Puritans and occultists, and I shall have occasion to say a great deal about it in the course of this chapter. Swift's reference to "the learned Dr. Henry More" and the tone of his note make abundantly clear the sympathy with which he read the pamphlet by More which was to play so important a part in *A Tale of a Tub.*

We know then that at the time he was writing his religious satire at Kilroot, if not earlier, Swift had been reading with sym-pathy at least two of the most important productions of the Angli-can rationalists: Stillingfleet's polemic against the Catholics and More's scathing attack upon the enthusiasm of the Puritans and occultists. This is all the evidence we have for such reading at this time, but we do have several other pieces of later evidence for his sympathy toward, and interest in, various Anglican rationalists.

In his *Remarks upon a Book Intitled "The Rights of the Christian Church"* (1708), an answer to Matthew Tindal, the deist, Swift spiritedly defends Stillingfleet from the aspersions Tindal had made on "the Character of that Prelate" (II, 79). Again, in his *Letter to a Young Gentleman Lately Entered into Holy Orders* (1720), there is a passage reflecting Swift's genuine admiration for Tillotson, whom he describes as "that excellent Prelate" (IX, 67). The catalogue of Swift's library drawn up in 1715 does not include, for a clergyman's library, a particularly large number of religious works in proportion to the total number of books included.[3] Some sixty-five works out of more than four hundred can be described as religious if we include ecclesiastical histories, scriptural exegeses, and devotional works. Yet a surprising number of the most important writings of the Anglican rationalists are included, such as Tillotson's *Works*, Cudworth's *True Intellectual System*, two volumes identified only as "Dr. Henry More's Tracts," and the works of such earlier rationalists as John Hales and William Chillingworth. Hooker, of course, is also included in this list. How early Swift had read Hooker we do not know, but in a contribution to the *Tatler* in 1710 he recommends "the Writings of *Hooker*" for their excellent style (II, 177).

One other reference by Swift to two of the Anglican rationalists has been cited, in support of their hypothesis that Swift distrusted the rationalist divines for employing reason in support of religion, by several commentators who regard Swift as a fideist. This occurs in *Mr. Collins's Discourse of Free-Thinking, Put into Plain English, by Way of Abstract, for the Use of the Poor* (1713), where More and Tillotson are several times referred to as "free-thinkers." Those who cite these passages treat them as serious statements by Swift himself. To do so is not only to miss Swift's irony but completely to overlook the fact that this is a highly amusing parody of Anthony Collins' book and is ostensibly written by one of Collins' friends and fellow deists. The whole effect of Swift's satire depends upon the way in which he parodies the logic of Collins and the other deists. If we were to take this logic as Swift's own, we should have to convict him of incredible stupidity. In the first passage which refers to More and Tillotson, the author, Collins' "friend," declares that these two divines, "both *Free-thinkers*,"

---

[3] Reprinted by T. P. Le Fanu in the *Proceedings of the Royal Irish Academy*, XXXVII, Sec. C (1927), 269–73.

differ from other divines on the interpretation of some of the parts of Scripture. Therefore, Collins' "friend" concludes, this gives him the right "to *think freely* for himself," for "suppose *Moor* and *Tillotson* deny the Eternity of Hell Torments, a *Free Thinker* may deny all future Punishments whatsoever" (IV, 34–35). Swift was fond of ridiculing this fallacy which he attributed to the reasoning of the deists. In *An Argument against Abolishing Christianity* (1708), he ascribed the same kind of false logic to the deists, pointing out that

> the Free-Thinkers consider [Christianity] as a Sort of Edifice, wherein all the Parts have such a mutual Dependance on each other, that if you happen to pull out one single Nail, the whole Fabrick must fall to the Ground. This was happily expressed by him, who had heard of a Text brought for Proof of the Trinity, which in an antient Manuscript was differently read; he thereupon immediately took the Hint, and by a sudden Deduction of a long *Sorites*, most logically concluded; Why, if it be as you say, I may safely whore and drink on, and defy the Parson [II, 38].

The other and longer passage is one in which Collins' "friend" attempts to show, by a specious and distorted interpretation of their teachings, that Socrates, Plato, Cicero, Solomon, the Prophets of the Old Testament, and Tillotson, along with a great many others, were all free-thinkers.[4] To attempt to prove that this is another example of fallacious logic would be to labor the obvious.

Swift's parable of the three brothers in *A Tale of a Tub* and the ornamental episodes connected with Peter's adventures employ conventions which are so common to Anglican rationalist polemics that it is hopeless to try to trace their source to any particular book by a member of the group. Stillingfleet's *Rational Account*, which we have seen he was acquainted with, may very

[4] See *The Prose Works of Jonathan Swift*, ed. Herbert Davis (Oxford, 1939—), IV, 41–47. For a very good discussion of the peculiar kind of irony employed in this satire, that of the "spurious enthymeme," see John M. Bullitt, *Jonathan Swift and the Anatomy of Satire* (Cambridge, Mass., 1953), pp. 97–104. For interpretations of this satire as a serious indictment of More and Tillotson as "freethinkers," see Ernest Tuveson, "Swift and the World Makers," *Journal of the History of Ideas*, XI (1950), 69; Kathleen Williams, *Jonathan Swift and the Age of Compromise* (Lawrence, Kan., 1958) p. 30.

well have contributed a part of these conventions, but there is no reason to suppose he was unacquainted at the time he wrote his religious satire with the polemics against Catholicism of some of the other members of this group or that he might not have drawn equally upon the sermons of Tillotson, the most famous preacher of the day. And for the over-all role he assigns to Jack in his parable, setting aside the ornamental episodes, Swift need not have gone farther than to Hooker. Besides, what is particularly effective about these passages is not the conventions themselves but the way in which Swift uses them in a parable which is his own invention. As employed by the Anglican rationalists, these conventions are merely static and humorless invectives against their Puritan and Catholic opponents. In employing these conventions by way of a parable, Swift enhances them in several ways. In the first place, what had appeared as mere statements by the Anglican rationalists as to the characteristic roles played by the three churches in the history of Christianity is rendered dramatically by the three brothers in speeches in which they disclose their views. Secondly, Swift is able through his parable to transform the humorless invective of these sermons and discourses into a dramatic presentation of the ridiculous behavior of two of the brothers which bears out and illustrates their theories at the same time that it induces the reader to laugh at their theories through their behavior.

Most readers, however, have found Jack far more laughable than Peter. This is largely because Jack is presented as irrational, while Peter is not. Peter's part in the story does not turn upon his folly, nor upon that of his brothers when they are living under his roof. Peter, as a clever mountebank who imposes various doctrines upon his brothers to serve his own ends, is anything but irrational. The dogmas, but not their author, are presented as irrational. Again, the brothers whom he intimidates are not irrational. They are simply deprived of all opportunity of exercising their reason. The spectacle of the brothers' plight and of Peter's behavior is comic, therefore, only in that it is outrageous.

The later comic behavior of Jack is of an altogether different kind. Jack's antics are far more laughable than Peter's because of his progressively irrational behavior which ends in madness. And this madness becomes the major theme of the later sections of the religious satire in *A Tale of a Tub*. If we examine the ornamental episodes concerning Jack, as well as the other parts of the religious satire in which madness appears, we will discover that in these places Swift was doing more than merely expressing the point of view and adopting the conventions of invective common to the Anglican rationalists as a whole and which required considerable changes in treatment to serve Swift's purpose of comic satire. In these places, it will appear, he has taken over comic devices themselves for which he was indebted in part at least to "the learned Dr. Henry More," whose *Enthusiasmus Triumphatus,* as we have seen, he had been reading at the time he wrote his satire on abuses in religion, if not earlier.

Jack's madness is not essential to Swift's parable itself; it is the basis for the ornamental episodes which portray his ridiculous behavior. Indeed, only after the history of Christianity, which it is the purpose of Swift's parable to relate, has been concluded in Section VI, does he become mad. He succeeds in reducing his coat to tatters (debasing the Christian religion), not because he is mad — this only comes afterwards — but because in his zeal to carry out the directions in his father's will he is unwilling to concede that his reason must provide him with the means of interpreting these directions and applying them to the restoration of his coat. Once this contrast between Martin's and Jack's wholly different methods of interpreting the will and treating their coats has been dramatized, the narrative itself comes to a close. Peter and Martin, the coats and the will recede into the background. All that survives of the parable is one of its characters, Jack, while the narration of a chronological succession of incidents which has brought the story down to Swift's own day gives place to a topical arrangement of ornamental episodes in Section XI which portray Jack's ridiculous behavior after he has gone mad. But, before these episodes can be presented, it must first of all be established that they all stem from the same disorder and that this disorder is madness in its most literal meaning.

Consequently, at the end of Section VI when the narrative itself comes to a close with a rupture between Martin and Jack which is as conclusive as their previous break with Peter, we are told that within a few days of this event "it was for certain reported, that [Jack] had run out of his Wits. In a short time after, he appeared abroad, and confirmed the Report, by falling into the oddest Whimsies that ever a sick Brain conceived" (I, 88). As a direct result of this disorder, the section concludes, "he hath given Rise to the most Illustrious and Epidemick Sect of *Aeolists,* who with honourable Commemoration, do still acknowledge the Renowned *Jack* for their Author and Founder" (I, 89). Not content with having grown mad himself, Jack has attracted to himself a rabble of frenzied men and organized them into a sect, complete with a system of belief and a code of behavior.

Section VIII is devoted entirely to a description of this sect of Aeolists founded by Jack. Swift begins by describing their system of beliefs, which turns entirely upon their reducing everything in the universe to the single principle of air, or wind. He then proceeds to describe the practices of this sect which grow out of their beliefs. These practices are simply various ways in which the Aeolists contrive to horde or to displode among the faithful the wind which they worship as the cause of all things.

It is perfectly clear to every reader that, in describing the sect of the Aeolists founded by Jack, Swift is satirizing the Puritans. And his description of the practices of the Aeolists is a clearly recognizable, though egregiously exaggerated, picture of those aspects of Puritan worship, especially preaching and public prayer, which were frequently derided by their enemies. It is not the practices of the Aeolists but their system of belief which raises difficulties for the reader of Swift's satire. For, in the first place, Swift describes this system of belief entirely in terms which are associated, not with Puritanism, but with occultism, as Guthkelch and Nichol Smith noticed and commented on in their edition of *A Tale of a Tub.* And by using "wind" as an ambiguous middle term standing both for "spirit" or "inspiration" as emphasized by the Puritans and for the "*anima mundi*" as emphasized by the occultists, Swift is offering the reader amusement at the expense of both Puritans and occultists by identifying the two. In telling us of the wind worshipped by the Aeolists that "this is what the *Adepti* [occultists] understand by their *Anima Mundi*; that is to say, the *Spirit, or Breath,* or *Wind* of the World" (I, 95), and then proceeding to present the religious worship of these same Aeolists as a parody of the Puritan emphasis in preaching and prayer alike upon inspiration or the guidance of the "Spirit," Swift is using Aeolism as the undistributed middle term of an amusing syllogism:

> All occultists are Aeolists.
> The Puritans are Aeolists.
> Therefore, the Puritans are occultists.

The questions which the reader wants answered at this point are what the occultists are doing in a religious satire and whether there was any basis for joining them with the Puritans in this way as sharing membership in the same mad sect. The answers are to be found by following Swift's hint and turning to the quarrel between Henry More and Thomas Vaughan, the occultist.

In 1650, Thomas Vaughan, who was a Rosicrucian and a brother of the poet Henry Vaughan, published a group of cabalistic tracts, two of which, *Anthroposophia Theomagica* and *Anima Magica Abscondita*, came to More's attention. In these tracts Vaughan, writing under the pseudonym of "Eugenius Philalethes," professed to offer his readers the true Platonic philosophy. But this "true Platonism" consisted in reality of the worst excesses of mystico-magical occultism. More's annoyance was understandable. One of the most prominent of the Cambridge Platonists, he was unwilling to watch in silence while Platonism was made to appear ridiculous in occultist dress. Accordingly, he answered Vaughan the same year, using the pseudonym "Alazonomastix Philalethes," in a pamphlet entitled *Observations upon Anthroposophia Theomagica and Anima Magica Abscondita*. When this drew an answer from Vaughan, called *The Man Mouse Taken in a Trap*, More replied the next year (1651) in another pamphlet, entitled *The Second Lash of Alazonomastix*.[5]

More realized that in answering Vaughan it would be a mistake to enter into a serious argument with such an adversary. In his efforts to revive Platonism, More had been motivated by religious considerations, and he had drawn freely upon such neo-Platonic commentators as Proclus and Plotinus in order to throw light upon religious matters. Vaughan also was trying to elucidate religion, and, in employing for this purpose the least creditable aspects of neo-Platonism, he had succeeded in producing what looked like a bad parody of More's writings. More's course, then, was not to discuss Vaughan's fantastic theories but to dissociate himself as much as possible from his imitator by discrediting him as a madman. The "Impulsive of writing" against him, he told Vaughan in his second pamphlet,

> was onely this; That you so carelessly and confidently adventuring upon the *Platonick* way, with so much tainted heat

[5] For further details of the controversy, see Marjorie Nicolson (ed.), *Conway Letters* (New Haven, Conn. 1930), pp. 72–73.

and distemper, that to my better composed spirit you seemed not a little disturbed in your phansie, and your bloud to be too hot to be sufficiently rectified by your brain, I thought it safe for me to keep those Books I wrote out of a spirit of sobernesse from reprochfull mistake: For your pretending the same way that I seem to be in, . . . there being no body else besides us two dealing with these kinds of notions, they might yoke me with so disordered a companion as your self.[6]

More's method of dealing with Vaughan, therefore, was to adopt an amused and slightly contemptuous tone toward his antagonist and to ridicule him as a "bestrid *Pythonick* or hackneyed *Enthusiastick*."[7]

Five years later, in 1656, More reissued his two tracts in answer to Vaughan as a single pamphlet. The immediate occasion for which they had been written had of course passed by this time. More felt, nevertheless, that they were worth reissuing, not because they were broadsides against Vaughan, but because through Vaughan he had exposed enthusiasm. He described his answer to Vaughan now as "those two Pamphlets against *Enthusiasme*" which were "very serviceable for that purpose intended them, *viz.* for the discountenancing and quelling of vain *Fantastry* and *Enthusiasme*."[8]

In order to justify the wider purpose he now attributed to his answer to Vaughan, More added a preface to his new pamphlet entitled "Enthusiasmus Triumphatus, or A Discourse of the Nature, Causes, Kinds, and Cure of Enthusiasme," for which he used the new pseudonym of "Philophilus Parresiastes." This was intended as a general discourse on enthusiasm which would serve as an introduction to the attacks on a particular enthusiast which followed. "Having undertaken the republishing of the two following Books," he wrote, "and reduced them both under one common Title of *Enthusiasme*, I think it not amisse to speak somewhat by way of Preface, concerning the nature of that Disease."[9]

We shall see later what More had to say of the nature and causes

[6] *The Second Lash of Alazonomastix* (Cambridge, 1651), pp. 35–36.
[7] *Ibid.*, p. 36.
[8] *Enthusiasmus Triumphatus* (London, 1656), "To the Reader," sig. A3v.
[9] *Ibid.*, p. 1.

of enthusiasm. Here it is what he has to say of the kinds of enthusiasm that is important. From the very beginning of his discourse it is clear that "enthusiasm" in this new context is a disorder shared by others besides the occultists, since More's frequent examples of enthusiasm include many of the Puritan sects, such as the Anabaptists and the Quakers. When he comes to a formal division of enthusiasm, which he has already defined as a "misconceit of being *inspired*," More suggests that there are two principal kinds of enthusiasm. "Wherefore setting aside all accuracie, we shall content our selves to distribute it, from the condition of the Persons in which it resides, into *Political* and *Philosophical*." [10] Enthusiasm is one or the other of these two kinds depending upon whether the "condition" of the person who suffers from "a misconceit of being inspired" leads him to give his zeal public or private expression.

Enthusiasm becomes political when the enthusiast takes it into his head to subvert whole kingdoms for the sake of his religious zeal and imagines himself called by God to set up a government of the "Saints," as in the case of John of Leyden and the recent founders of the Commonwealth or, to use More's most lengthy example, the notorious David George, who in the previous century had founded the sect of "Davidists" on the Continent. "Wherefore those whose Temper carries them most to *Political* affairs, who love rule and honour . . . sometimes fancy themselves great Princes (at least by divine assignment) and Deliverers of the people sent from God." [11] All of the instances of "political" enthusiasts offered by More were founders of religious sects which in England under the name of Puritans and on the Continent under various other names had been the cause of so much political disturbance since the Reformation.

In less active spirits, whose temper disposes them to confine their religious zeal to private bounds, enthusiasm takes the form of occultism, causing somewhat less disturbance to the community. "THAT *other kinde* of *Enthusiasm* I propounded was *Philosophical*," More writes, "because found in such as are of a more

[10] "Enthusiasmus Triumphatus," *A Collection of Several Philosophical Writings of Dr. Henry More, Fellow of Christ's Colledge in Cambridge* (2d ed.; London, 1662), p. 22. All references to *Enthusiasmus Triumphatus* hereafter will be taken from this far more accessible edition.
[11] *Ibid.*

Speculative and *Philosophical* complexion." [12] More draws all of his examples of "philosophical" enthusiasts from various notorious occultists and theosophists. And he devotes as much attention to Paracelsus, as a typical occultist, as he had given to David George, as a typical religious fanatic. The occultists, More points out, are religious enthusiasts quite as much as are the sectarian fanatics, for being

> prone to Religion and devotion, as well as to the curious Con-
> templation of things, these natural motions and affections to-
> wards God may drive them to a belief that he has a more then
> ordinary affection towards them, and that they have so special
> an assistance and guidance from him, nay such a mysterious,
> but intimate and real, union with him, that every fine thought
> or fancy that steals into their mind ought to be look't upon
> by them as a pledge of the Divine favour, and a singular il-
> lumination from God himself." [13]

In reading More's answer to Vaughan, then, Swift came upon an effective and often amusing discourse against enthusiasm which associated the fanatics with the occultists as similar victims of religious delusion. And, when he came to write Section VIII of *A Tale of a Tub,* he likewise associated the two under the common name of Aeolists, by which, he indicated in a note, he meant *"All Pretenders to Inspiration whatsoever"* (I, 95). But he is not, properly speaking, satirizing the occultists. If satire is the attempt to degrade an individual or group, it is pointless to satirize an individual or group already regarded by the public as beneath contempt. Furthermore, to associate two groups considered respectable by some at least of the satirist's readers is to degrade neither of them. If, on the other hand, the satirist can associate his victims with a group already regarded as contemptible, he will succeed in making his victims appear contemptible as well. "Occultist" was a term of contempt to most people in the seventeenth century, and the haste with which More had moved to dissociate himself from an occultist such as Vaughan is understandable. Swift could scarcely have ridiculed the Puritans more effectively than by associating them with the occultists in his sect of the Aeolists. He did not soon forget how useful the occultists could be as a contempti-

[12] *Ibid.,* p. 28.
[13] *Ibid.,* pp. 28–29.

ble group with whom to associate others whom he wished to ridicule. Later, when he came to write the sections of *A Tale of a Tub* in which he satirized abuses in learning, he associated the occultists with the Moderns again and again.[14]

Swift does more, however, than simply associate the religious fanatics with the occultists, as More had done, in his presentation of the sect of the Aeolists. He identifies the two, as we have seen, by using Aeolism itself as an ambiguous middle term, and this raises another difficulty for the reader. In describing Aeolism as a philosophical system, he distorts the theories of the occultists quite as much as he does the beliefs of the Puritans. To emphasize the *anima mundi* in the manner of the occultists, or the importance of inspiration in the manner of the Puritans, is one thing; to make this spirit or "wind" the principle of the entire universe is quite another matter. Furthermore, neither occultism nor Puritanism can properly be described as a philosophical system. It is possible, of course, that Swift is taking aim at a secondary target here which is philosophical rather than religious. But before we conclude that Swift could not have been aiming at the Puritans by describing a philosophical system, Aeolism will have to be examined more closely.

What is significant about Aeolism is not simply the fact that it is a philosophical system. Its peculiar characteristic is that it is a reductive system, that is to say, it reduces the entire universe to a single principle, in this case air or wind, which is used as an explanation for anything that comes under the philosopher's observation. Air or wind is "the ruling *Element* in every Compound," "the Original Cause of all Things," the principle of corruption in everything and, finally, "Life itself" (I, 95). The problem, then, is not whether occultism and religious fanaticism are correctly described as a philosophy but whether enthusiasm, which More had pictured as the common characteristic of occultism and fanaticism, can be appropriately ridiculed as a reductive system. The answer to this problem, I should like to suggest, can be found in one of Hooker's cleverest characterizations of Puritanism.

[14] See, for example, *Prose Works*, I, 34–35, 41–42, 78–79, 118–19. Miriam K. Starkman discusses Swift's association of the occultists with the Moderns in *Swift's Satire on Learning in "A Tale of a Tub"* (Princeton, N.J., 1950), pp. 44–56.

In the long preface to his famous book, Hooker permitted himself greater freedom in handling the Puritans than he considered appropriate in the *Laws* itself. At one point he describes at some length the extravagances to which their "zeal for the cause" led the Puritans. He notes:

> Pythagoras, by bringing up his scholars in the speculative knowledge of numbers, made their conceits therein so strong, that when they came to the contemplation of things natural, they imagined that in every particular thing they even beheld as it were with their eyes, how the elements of number gave essence and being to the works of nature: a thing in reason impossible; which notwithstanding, through their misfashioned preconceit, appeared unto them no less certain, than if nature had written it in the very foreheads of all the creatures of God ["Preface," iii, 9].

The situation of the Puritans, Hooker suggests, is analogous to that of Pythagoras' scholars, for in their zeal, so strong is their "misfashioned preconceit" of being inspired, that they imagine all manner of things which are "in reason impossible."

Swift's problem, I suggest, in creating the sect of the Aeolists, was to combine two very effective devices for satirizing enthusiasm which he had met with in his reading: More's association of the fanatics with the equally enthusiastic and far more contemptible occultists and Hooker's suggestion of the close analogy between Puritan enthusiasm and the reductive systems of some philosophers. The effective solution of Swift's problem lay in his discovering a reductive system whose single principle of explanation was one which could be stretched in such a way as to be applicable to some central belief of each of the two groups he wished to associate. In this way he could identify the fanatics with the occultists far more closely than More had done, by using this single principle as an ambiguous middle term and, at the same time, he could make the Puritans actual believers in a reductive system which Hooker had only suggested as analogous to their enthusiasm. Swift could have invented such a reductive system; but in fact he did not. He did not have to invent a reductive system whose single principle of explanation was air or wind, which would appropriately serve for both the occultist *anima mundi* and the Puritan's inspiration. It had been invented long before.

It required no very close acquaintance with the history of philosophy, once Swift had hit upon air or wind as a middle term appropriate to both the occultists and the Puritans, to recall that air was one of the four elements of the ancient world and that a characteristic of several of the pre-Socratic philosophers was that they constructed reductive systems by making one or the other of these four elements the principle of the universe. Thus Heraclitus founded his whole system upon the element of fire, while Thales found a similar explanation for the universe in the element of water. But it was Anaximenes who constructed a reductive system by making the element of air the principle of all things.

The only question remaining is how the system of Anaximenes could have come to the attention of Swift, who, at the prospect of having to read for an examination at Oxford, wrote his cousin in 1692: "To enter upon causes of Philosophy is what I protest I will rather die in a ditch than go about." [15] The easiest and most obvious source where one might learn at a glance the basic teachings of any philosopher was at that time Thomas Stanley's *History of Philosophy*. First published between 1655 and 1662, Stanley's book became popular immediately and by 1690 had gone through several editions and had been translated into Latin on the Continent. It carries the subtitle of "The Lives, Opinions, Actions and Discourses of the Philosophers of Every Sect" and is essentially a work of reference rather than a history, for it consists of a series of encyclopedic articles on the philosophers, arranged in chronological sequence. It is provided with a remarkably detailed table of contents from which the casual reader can learn at a glance the characteristic features of each philosophical sect. It is almost impossible to doubt that it was in Stanley's *History of Philosophy*, in the article on Anaximenes, that Swift found his sect of the Aeolists, for he closely paraphrased several of Stanley's sentences, I suggest, in his own account of the Aeolists, simply changing "air" to "wind". Swift's description of the Aeolists begins: "THE Learned *Aeolists*, maintain the Original Cause of all Things to be *Wind*, from which Principle this whole Universe was at first produced, and into which it must at last be resolved" (I, 95). Stanley's description of Anaximenes' opinions commences: "He held that the *Air is the Principle of the Universe, of which all things are en-*

66

gendred, and into which they resolve." [16] Swift proceeds next to establish an equation between this air or wind and "spirit," so that the Aeolist principle will apply equally to the occultist *anima mundi* and Puritan inspiration: "For, whether you please to call the *Forma informans* of Man, by the Name of *Spiritus, Animus, Afflatus,* or *Anima*; What are all these but several Appellations for *Wind*?" If we continue with Stanley's account of the system of Anaximenes, we read: *"Our Souls by which we live are Air, so Spirit and Air contain in being all the World, for Spirit and Air are two names signifying one thing."*

These, then, are the elements, I suggest, out of which Swift constructed his sect of the Aeolists. If the elements themselves were not original, it was nevertheless a stroke of genius on Swift's part to combine them in the way he did to satirize the beliefs of the Puritans. Furthermore, the system Swift probably discovered in Stanley's *History of Philosophy* was also peculiarly appropriate as a means of ridiculing the religious practices of the Puritans, as will appear when I come to Swift's presentation of the cause of enthusiasm.

When Swift has completed his description of the sect of the Aeolists to which Section VIII is entirely devoted, he begins Section IX, the "Digression concerning Madness," with these words:

> Nor shall it any ways detract from the just Reputation of this famous Sect, that its Rise and Institution are owing to such an Author as I have described *Jack* to be; A Person whose Intellectuals were overturned, and his Brain shaken out of its Natural Position; which we commonly suppose to be a Distemper, and call by the Name of *Madness* or *Phrenzy* [I, 102].

The madness of their founder is no disgrace to the Aeolists, he tells us, because the three "greatest Actions that have been performed in the World, under the Influence of Single Men," one of which is *"the contriving, as well as the propagating of New Religions,"* have all had madmen for their authors. After a detailed description of the two other greatest actions, which I shall examine

[16] *The History of Philosophy: Containing the Lives, Opinions, Actions and Discourses of the Philosophers of Every Sect* (3rd ed.; London, 1701), p. 62.

later in this chapter, Swift returns briefly to the Aeolists, whom he
has already discussed fully in the preceding section, and remarks:

> Whosoever pleases to look into the Fountains of *Enthusi-
> asm*, from whence, in all Ages, have eternally proceeded such
> fatning Streams, will find the Spring Head to have been as
> *troubled* and *muddy* as the Current; Of such great Emolu-
> ment, is a Tincture of this *Vapour*, which the World calls
> *Madness*, that without its Help . . . all Mankind would un-
> happily be reduced to the same Belief in Things Invisible
> [I, 107].

Swift then proceeds to explain at length the causes of the madness which religious enthusiasm shares with the two other "greatest actions that have been performed in the world." Finally, having
told us that Jack is mad and explained why he is mad, in Section
XI Swift concludes his account of the last of the brothers by showing his madness in action. These ornamental episodes, in which
Jack engages in various forms of frenzy, have recognizable counterparts in different aspects of Puritan belief and practice. Jack's
bedlamite antics are sufficiently amusing even today. At the time
they were written, when admission was still being charged and
willingly paid to see the "sights" of Bedlam, they were a far more
effective means of making the Puritans appear ridiculous.

As a hyperbole for describing their rejection of reason in religion,
the ascription of madness to the religious fanatics is so obviously
appropriate that it is easy to suppose Swift invented it. Yet important as madness undoubtedly is as Swift's principal means of
ridiculing the Puritans, it almost certainly owes its presence in *A
Tale of a Tub* to Swift's reading of More's answer to Vaughan,
Enthusiasmus Triumphatus, particularly of the preface to that
pamphlet.

As More presents enthusiasm in his discourse on the subject, it
is, by its very definition, nothing short of madness. For he defines
enthusiasm as "a misconceit of being inspired," and no man, he
insists, is capable of such gross self-deception unless he be mad.
If the fanatics and occultists share the same enthusiasm, so also
they share the same madness, for, say what you will in their defense, "as for this one particular of being *supernaturally inspired*
. . . this certainly in them is as true, but farre worse, dotage, then

to fancy a mans self either a *Cock* or *Bull*, when it is plain to the senses of all that he is a *Man*."[17] And the more he warms to his subject, the more he uses "dotage," "frenzy," and "madness" as synonyms for enthusiasm and indulges his vein for ridicule at the expense of the fanatics and occultists. For scathing wit, no other polemic of the Anglican rationalists can approach *Enthusiasmus Triumphatus*.

If More's discourse on enthusiasm was never equalled, it was often imitated by his friends, and within a few years of its appearance the method devised by More for ridiculing the fanatics had become a characteristic feature of Anglican rationalist polemics. Hallywell wrote a book against the Quakers in which he pictured them as madmen, Rust similarly described the Puritans, and Glanvill exploited the madness of the fanatics incessantly.

> The way to be a *Christian* [he wrote on one of these frequent occasions] is *first* to be a *Brute*; and to be a *true Believer,* in *this Divinity*, is to be *fit for Bedlam*. . . . So that if a man would recommend any thing, for his life, to those *enemies* of *Reason*, it must be some odd *non-sense*, in the cloathing of *Imagination*; and he that can be the *Author* of a *new* kind of *madness*, shall *lead a Party*.[18]

As a means of ridiculing the Puritans, madness was well worth exploiting, and Glanvill and Hallywell both acknowledged their debt to More's invention.

The question naturally arises why the Anglican rationalists had taken to ridiculing the Puritans. Ridicule is not often successful as a means of persuasion, and few men have been converted by being laughed at as mad. The answer is to be found in the radical change in the climate of apologetics between Hooker's day and the era following the Restoration. When Hooker wrote his reasonable appeal to the anti-episcopal party, the lines dividing the two parties were still fluid and the Puritans still were members of the Established Church. There was hope yet that the two parties could

---

[17] *Enthusiasmus Triumphatus*, p. 10.
[18] *Philosophia Pia* (London, 1671), pp. 223–24. See also Hallywell, *An Account of Familism, as It is Revived and Propagated by the Quakers* (London, 1673), pp. 104–11; Rust, *Discourse of the Use of Reason* (London, 1683), p. 33.

settle their differences and restore harmony to the national church. But the situation a century later was far different. After the Act of Uniformity was passed in 1662, the Puritans had been excluded from the Church of England, and what had once been difference of discipline now became permanent dissent. As far as the Anglican rationalists were concerned, the Puritans were hopeless, and all appeals to them ceased. They were still a source of danger to the church, but of a different kind. They could no longer subvert the Establishment as they once had threatened to do, but by their unmistakable religious zeal they could attract others into dissent. And this was the danger the Anglican rationalists tried to meet by ridiculing the Puritans before the Anglican faithful, holding them up as objects of derision whom no sane man would follow.

Now ridicule of the Puritans was not new, nor was it the peculiar property of the Anglican rationalists. It had appeared at least as early as Ben Jonson's Zeal-of-the-Land Busy and had become a comic convention long before More turned his attention to the religious fanatics. Nor were the Anglican rationalists the only clergymen of their church who employed ridicule to stop the spread of nonconformity. But there is an important difference between the usual way of ridiculing fanaticism and the method which the Anglican rationalists made their own. It is as wide as the difference between hypocrisy and madness, between a Tartuffe and Jack as he appears in *A Tale of a Tub*. The standard and eventually monotonous way of ridiculing the Puritans in plays, poems, and pamphlets from one end of the seventeenth century to the other was to portray them as bores, busybodies, and troublemakers who were essentially hypocrites in that they pretended to an inspiration which they knew themselves was counterfeit. Their enthusiasm was pictured not as a "misconceit of being inspired" but as a pretension to being inspired, and the fanatics themselves were consequently treated not as madmen but as charlatans. Some years ago, C. M. Webster offered striking evidence of the extent to which most Englishmen accepted this picture of the Puritans as hypocrites. After reading several hundred polemics against the Puritans published in the seventeenth century, he reported that the only writers after the Restoration who pictured the Puritans as sincere victims of delusion were Meric Casaubon, More, and the anonymous authors of two pamphlets influenced by More, while the only such writer earlier in the century was Robert Burton, whose influence upon More I shall discuss later.[19] Webster's study was not exhaustive, for he overlooked the similar way in which Glanvill, Rust, and Hallywell portrayed the fanatics.[20] But it shows unmistakably how unusual was the method the Anglican rationalists used for ridiculing the Puritans, and it is curious that its implications were never explored by commentators on *A Tale of a Tub*.

The Anglican rationalists did not abandon the conventional means of ridiculing the fanatics simply because it was becoming hackneyed. They rejected hypocrisy as an explanation for the zeal of the Puritans because they felt that as a means of accounting for enthusiasm it was false and as a way of picturing the Puritans to the Anglican faithful it was unwise. Glanvill spoke for the Anglican rationalists as a whole when he declared that, although the Puritans were not truly inspired, they "yet are not to be reckon'd *Hypocritical Impostors*, for they infinitely believe themselves, and the *strength* of their highly invigorated fancies shuts out the sober *light* of Reason that should dis-abuse them, as *sleep* doth that of our external senses in our *dreams*." [21] To picture the fanatics as hypocrites when they were really sincere was not only false but ineffectual as a means of discouraging the growth of dissent.

There is nothing whereby the common people are drawn more easily into the ways of *Sects* and *Separations* [he pointed

[19] See "Swift's *Tale of a Tub* Compared with Earlier Satires of the Puritans," *PMLA*, XLVII (1932), 171–78. See also the same author's "Swift and Some Earlier Satirists of Puritan Enthusiasm," *PMLA*, XLVIII (1933), 1141–53, and "The Satiric Background of the Attack on the Puritans in Swift's *A Tale of a Tub*," *PMLA*, L (1935), 210–23. The two pamphlets mentioned by Webster are *Semper Eidem; or, A Parallel betwixt the Ancient and Modern Fanatics* (1661) and *The Life and Death of Ralph Wallis, the Cobler of Gloucester* (1670). The attacks upon enthusiasm of Casaubon, More, and others are also discussed in George Williamson, "The Restoration Revolt against Enthusiasm," *Studies in Philology*, XXX (1933), 571–603, and Truman Guy Steffan, "The Social Argument against Enthusiasm (1650–1660)," in *Studies in English* (Austin, Tex., 1941), pp. 39–63.
[20] The first to draw attention to Glanvill's portrayal of the Puritans as sincere "deluded people" was Jackson I. Cope in "Joseph Glanvill, Anglican Apologist: Old Ideas and New Style in the Restoration," *PMLA*, LXIX (1954), 223–50, and in his recent book, *Joseph Glanvill: Anglican Apologist* (St. Louis, Mo., 1956).
[21] *Philosophia Pia*, p. 59.

out] then by the observation of the *zeal* and *devotion* of *those*
of the *factions*. . . . For the generality of men are tempted
into *Schism* and *Parties*, not so much by the *arguments* of
Fanaticks, as by the *opinion* of their *Godliness*.

It was useless, therefore, for the Anglican clergy to tell their people
that the Puritans were only feigning zeal, "for many of them
know, that they are in *earnest*, and consequently that their op-
posers are mistaken in their judgments concerning them." The
more effective way of disabusing the common people, then, would
be to take a quite different approach to the Puritans, as Glanvill
pointed out, and to

grant to them that they may be *serious,* believe themselves
infinitely, and feel all those Warmths, which they pretend,
and yet be *evil men*, and far enough from being *godly* [since]
all their *zeal* and *Devotion*, and more and greater than *theirs*,
may arise from a principle that hath nothing *Divine* and
supernatural in it.[22]

The first Anglican divine who attempted to show that the zeal
of the Puritans arose "from a principle that hath nothing Divine
and supernatural in it" was Meric Casaubon, whose *Treatise concerning Enthusiasme* (1655) carries the subtitle: "As it is an Effect
of *Nature*: but is mistaken by many for either *Divine Inspiration*,
or *Diabolical Possession*." Casaubon was convinced of the Puritans' sincerity. He defined enthusiasm as "the opinion of divine
Inspiration," by which, he added, "I mean a real, though but imaginary, apprehension of it in the parties, upon some ground of
nature; a real, not barely pretended, counterfeit, and simulatory,
for politick ends."[23] Casaubon's purpose in his book is not to
ridicule the Puritans but to show that the sincere opinion of in-

[22] *The Way of Happiness* (London, 1670), pp. 145–49.
[23] *A Treatise concerning Enthusiasme* (London, 1655), p. 3. Casaubon was not an Anglican rationalist, although he shared their attitude
toward enthusiasm. Like many another Anglican clergyman, he could
appeal to reason in assailing Puritanism, Catholicism, or atheism, as
the occasion demanded. But apologetics was not his primary concern,
and he dissented from the Anglican rationalists in at least two important respects: their attitude toward the Royal Society, which I shall
discuss later in this chapter, and their theory of knowledge, which I
shall take up in chap. iv.

spiration shared by the fanatics has no supernatural source. He says nothing of madness but devotes his attention to finding a natural explanation for various kinds of "inspiration" mistakenly attributed to supernatural causes.

> My business therefore shall be, as by examples of all professions in all ages, to shew how men have been very prone upon some grounds of nature, producing some extraordinary though not supernaturall effects; really, not hypocritically, but yet falsely and erroniously, to deem themselves divinely inspired. . . . Of Religious *Enthusiasme*, [he later remarks,] truly and really religious, nothing will be found here.[24]

Casaubon proposed to discuss nine different kinds of "natural" enthusiasm in his book, but he published his book after treating only five of them. One of the kinds of enthusiasm he proposed but failed to discuss was "*Mechanical* Enthusiasme."

It is probable that Casaubon's treatise on enthusiasm gave More the idea of writing *Enthusiasmus Triumphatus* the following year, for he refers to the earlier book in his own discourse. He adopted Casaubon's view of the sincerity of the fanatics:

> For *Enthusiasme* is nothing else but a misconceit of being *inspired*. Now to be *inspired* is, *to be moved in an extraordinary manner by the power or Spirit of God to act, speak, or think what is holy, just and true.* From hence it will be easily understood what *Enthusiasm* is, viz. *A full, but false, perswasion in a man that he is inspired.*"[25]

Like Casaubon before him, More recognized Divine inspiration and diabolical possession as alternative kinds of enthusiasm but dismissed them as irrelevant to his subject, which was concerned with natural enthusiasm only. But More was not satisfied with following Casaubon's tedious method of producing lifeless arguments to show that there was a natural explanation for the "inspiration" of the fanatics. Instead, he carried Casaubon's thesis a step further and showed that if there was a natural explanation for the fanatics' delusion this explanation was to be found in madness. The lively and often humorous account to which he turned his explanation appealed to the imagination of other Anglican

[24] *Ibid.*, pp. 4, 19.
[25] *Enthusiasmus Triumphatus*, p. 2.

rationalists interested in exposing the Puritans, as we have seen, and it was More's clever embellishment of Casaubon's idea that they in turn employed, imitating *Enthusiasmus Triumphatus* with a freedom that amounted at times to plagiarism.[26] Like his predecessor, More speculated on the possibility of yet another kind of enthusiasm: mechanical. But after briefly mentioning it, he too dismissed mechanical enthusiasm, remarking: "But this kind of *Enthusiasm* I do not so much aim at as that which is *Natural.*" [27]

Here, then, was a ready-formulated and highly effective method of ridiculing the "inspiration" of the Puritans as an effect of nature and a by-product of madness which Swift could find in reading the answer to Vaughan of "the learned Dr. Henry More." In using this convention in *A Tale of a Tub*, he contributed, as usual, the spark of his own invention, substituting for More's citation of historical examples the even more effective method of dramatizing enthusiastic madness through the person and behavior of Jack. But not content with exploiting the dramatic possibilities of "natural enthusiasm" in *A Tale of a Tub* itself, Swift went further, and in *A Discourse concerning the Mechanical Operation of the Spirit*, appended as a "fragment" at the back of his book, he followed the hint provided by More and Casaubon and offered a devastating account of yet a fourth kind of enthusiasm, the mechanical, which his predecessors had mentioned but passed over in order to concentrate on natural enthusiasm. As it figures in religion, writes the imaginary author of the *The Mechanical Operation of the Spirit*, enthusiasm has

> produced certain Branches of a very different Nature, however often mistaken for each other. The Word in its universal Acceptation, may be defined, *A lifting up of the Soul or its Faculties above Matter.* This Description will hold good in general; but I am only to understand it, as applied to *Religion*; wherein there are three general Ways of ejaculating the

[26] Compare, for example, the following statement by Hallywell with the quotation from *Enthusiasmus Triumphatus* cited in this paragraph: "Now to be inspired is to be moved in an extraordinary manner by the Power or Spirit of God to act, speak or think what is holy, just, and true; from whence it follows, that Enthusiasm is a full but false Persuasion in a man that he is inspired" (*An Account of Familism.* pp. 104–5).

[27] *Enthusiasmus Triumphatus*, p. 21.

Soul, or transporting it beyond the Sphere of Matter. The first, is the immediate Act of God, and is called, *Prophecy* or *Inspiration*. The second, is the immediate Act of the Devil, and is termed *Possession*. The third, is the Product of natural Causes, the effect of strong Imagination, Spleen, violent Anger, Fear, Grief, Pain, and the like. These three have been abundantly treated on by Authors, and therefore shall not employ my Enquiry" [I, 174–75].

It will be noticed that these are the same three kinds of enthusiasm, the first two supernatural and the third natural, into which Casaubon and More had divided religious enthusiasm before proceeding to treat of the third. It is the fourth kind, however, which they had only suggested as a possibility, which is Swift's subject in his "fragment." "But, the fourth Method of *Religious Enthusiasm*, or launching out the Soul," the imaginary author writes, "as it is purely an Effect of Artifice and *Mechanick Operation*, has been sparingly handled, or not at all, by any Writer" (I, 175). It is this fourth method which he proceeds to discuss, pointing out that "I have said, that there is one Branch of *Religious Enthusiasm*, which is purely an Effect of Nature; whereas, the Part I mean to handle, is wholly an Effect of Art" (I, 175). In the discourse which follows, the imaginary author of the "fragment" offers an amusing account of the various ways in which the members of the Puritan congregations, who, unlike the founders of these sects, are not mad to begin with, can nevertheless manage to reproduce by artifice the same effects which their preachers owe entirely to nature.

We have seen how in his sect of the Aeolists Swift employed a reductive system of belief as a means of characterizing enthusiasm. In the sect of the tailor-worshippers described in Section II, he presents another reductive system. Whereas the Aeolists reduce the entire universe to the single principle of wind or air, the tailor-worshippers find such a principle of explanation in clothing. We are first told that this sect worships an idol, and Swift explains in a note that "*by this* Idol *is meant a Taylor*." The paragraph in which Swift describes their method of worshipping this idol is easily understood. It is simply an amusing account of the emphasis, amounting almost to worship, which the "*Grand Monde*" in every age gives to clothing and the importance they attach to dressing in the latest style. Swift's note to this paragraph reads: "*This is an Occasional Satyr upon Dress and Fashion, in order to introduce what follows*" (I, 46). "What follows," however, is something of an altogether different kind from the occasional satire by which it is introduced. Swift devotes the remainder of his discussion of the tailor-worshippers to an examination of the beliefs upon which they found their worship. He tells the reader that "the Worshippers of this Deity had also a System of their Belief, which seemed to turn upon the following Fundamental. They held the Universe to be a large *Suit of Cloaths*, which *invests* every Thing" (I, 46). It soon becomes apparent that the philosophers of this sect use clothing as the single principle of explanation for everything that comes under their observation in the same way that the Aeolists employed wind or air. Not only is the universe itself a suit of clothes, but every part of the universe, including "this Globe of Earth," both land and sea, and all the "particular Works of the Creation," even "Man himself," are all of them parts of this clothing "which invests everything."

There are two branches of these tailor-worshippers, Swift tells the reader, distinguished by their respective beliefs as to the nature of man. Some simply believed "that those Beings which the World calls improperly *Suits of Cloaths*, are in Reality the most refined Species of Animals, or to proceed higher, that they are Rational Creatures, or Men" (I, 47). But "others of these Professors, though agreeing in the main System, were yet more refined upon certain Branches of it; and held that Man was an Animal compounded of two *Dresses*, the *Natural* and the *Celestial Suit*, which were the Body and the Soul" (I, 48). To support their theory, this second group resorted to certain philosophical formulas, such as "*ex traduce*" and "*All in All, and All in every Part.*"

Swift did not annotate his description of the beliefs of the tailor-worshippers, and the part it plays in his religious satire is not immediately obvious to the modern reader. Yet he is clearly satirizing some definite target, and it is difficult to believe that for once he was so obscure that his contemporaries missed the whole point of his ridicule. A closer examination of the tailor-worshippers' system of belief can, I think, bring to light what it was that Swift was satirizing. All the evidence, I suggest, points to materialism as the object of his ridicule. In the first place, there is a logical connection of some kind, slight though it is, between the "occasional satire upon dress and fashion," offered by means of the devotional practices of the tailor-worshippers, and the system of belief underlying these practices. And an undue attention to such matters as dress to the exclusion of more important considerations is described even today as "materialistic." More important, however, is the part Swift's description of the tailor-worshippers and their beliefs plays in the context of the parable he is relating in Section II. They are introduced at that point in the history of Christianity when, after seven years of close attention to the directions of their father's will (seven centuries of genuine practice of the Christian religion), the three brothers, none of whom is yet distinguished by name, first begin to add ornaments to their coats (that is, to corrupt the Christian religion) in disobedience to their father's commands. And they do so as a direct result of their contact with the tailor-worshippers. The system of belief professed by the tailor-worshippers, then, is an antireligious doctrine in direct contradiction to Christianity. The literal antithesis of religion is materialism. Thirdly, the single principle itself to which the tailor-worshippers reduce everything and by which they seek to explain all existence is in direct, and obviously deliberate, contrast to the single principle on which the Aeolists depend. For the Aeolists all matter is airy and insubstantial since it is derived from wind, while on the contrary the tailor-worshippers regard everything that exists, even man's soul, as tangible and visible since it is all some form of clothing. Aeolism, we have seen, through an equation of wind or air with spirit, represents a tendency to see the "Spirit" in everything, even the most trivial of matters. The system of belief of the tailor-worshippers, I suggest, represents the opposite mistake of seeing spirit nowhere as a result of the insistence that everything in the universe is tangible and visible, as a result, in short, of materialism. Finally, although the technical terms Swift introduces into his account, such as "*ex traduce*" and "All in all, and all in every part," have been consistently ignored, and the latter formula has been incorrectly identified with the philosophy of Anaxagoras by Guthkelch and Nichol Smith, they are nevertheless significant. They serve the same purpose as the technical terms of occultism in the Aeolists' system, for they are clues to his meaning with which Swift has provided the reader. Both of these formulas are connected with theories concerning the human soul which, it can be shown, were regarded in Swift's day as lending support to materialism. Every hint which can be discovered in Swift's description of the beliefs of the tailor-worshippers, then, points unmistakably to materialism as the target of his satire.

There is an apparent difficulty in this interpretation. We have seen that the beliefs of the tailor-worshippers constitute a reductive system which is as monistic as that of the Aeolists, for both systems reduce the complex phenomena of existence to a simple and unique principle. We have also seen that Hooker pointed out the similarity between systems of this kind and enthusiasm and that Swift attributed a reductive system to the Aeolists in order to ridicule the enthusiasm shared by Puritans and occultists alike. If a reductive system as such represents enthusiasm in Section VIII, we have a right to expect that it should also represent enthusiasm in Section II, although the particular variety of enthusiasm will vary according to the individual system described. The obvious objection is that enthusiasm is a religious phenomenon which is as far as possible removed from the irreligious, and even atheistic, attitude described as materialism.

This is, in fact, the very objection raised by several readers of Shaftesbury's *Letter concerning Enthusiasm* when it appeared in 1708. Shaftesbury had remarked in his letter "that enthusiasm is wonderfully powerful and extensive; that it is a matter of nice judgment, and the hardest thing in the world to know fully and distinctly; since even atheism is not exempt from it. For, as some have well remarked, there have been enthusiastical atheists." [28] This statement was objected to, and in 1711 in his "Miscellaneous Reflections," published as part of the *Characteristicks*, Shaftesbury defended the connection he had suggested between atheism and enthusiasm by pointing out that he had merely been repeating an idea he had found in Cudworth's *True Intellectual System* and in More's *Enthusiasmus Triumphatus*.[29]

As early as 1652, four years before he wrote *Enthusiasmus Triumphatus*, More was writing of the "*neer alliance* and *mutuall correspondence* betwixt these two enormous distempers of the Mind, *Atheism* and *Enthusiasme*." In the preface to *An Antidote against Atheism*, he wrote:

> *Atheism* and *Enthusiasm*, though they seem so extremely opposite one to another, yet in many things they do very

[28] *Characteristics*, ed. John M. Robertson (London, 1900), I, 37.
[29] See *ibid.*, II, 196–98.

nearly agree. For to say nothing of their joynt conspiracy against the true knowledge of God and Religion, they are commonly entertain'd, though successively, in the same Complexion. For that temper that disposes a man to listen to the Magisterial Dictates of an over-bearing Fancy, more then to the calm and cautious insinuations of free Reason, is a subject that by turns does very easily lodge and give harbour to these mischievous Guests.[30]

The passage continues at some length, developing an idea which seems to have struck More's fancy. When he republished a number of his works as *A Collection of Several Philosophical Writings* in 1662, More printed *Enthusiasmus Triumphatus* as a companion piece to *An Antidote against Atheism,* justifying the new connection between the two discourses by substituting the passage from which I have just quoted for the original opening of *Enthusiasmus Triumphatus.* In this form it continued to be reprinted thereafter, with the statement that atheists and enthusiasts share the same "complexion" or "temper" followed by the explanation farther on in *Enthusiasmus Triumphatus* that this complexion or temper was madness, as we have already seen. As usual, More established a convention in this respect which other Anglican rationalists were not long in adopting.

Glanvill made this theme of the "near alliance" between atheism and enthusiasm a frequent subject of his discourses, stressing, like More, the fact that both were due to the same complexion or temper.[31] And when More's friend Cudworth finally published his *True Intellectual System* in 1678, he completed the process begun by More and promoted the alliance between atheism and enthusiasm into an identification, by writing of the "*Enthusiastical* or *Fanatical Atheists.*" He assured his readers that

all manner of Atheists whatsoever, and those of them who most of all pretend to Reason and Philosophy, may in some sence be justly stiled also both *Enthusiasts* and *Fanaticks.* Forasmuch as they are not led or carried on, into this way of Atheizing, by any clear Dictates of their Reason or Understanding, but only by . . . *a certain Blind and Irrational Impetus,* they being as it were *Inspired* to it. [Atheists are] no

[30] *An Antidote against Atheism* (2nd ed.; London, 1655), sig. A5.
[31] See, for example, his *Seasonable Reflections and Discourses* (London, 1676), pp. 150–51, and *Philosophia Pia,* p. 218.

better, than a kind of *Bewitched Enthusiasts* and *Blind Spiritati*, that are wholly ridden and acted by a dark, narrow and captivated Principle of Life, and, to use their own Language, *In-blown* by it, and by it bereft, even in Speculative things, of all Free Reason and Understanding.[32]

Swift employed a reductive system in Section II of *A Tale of a Tub*, then, to represent the same disorder it represented in Section VIII: enthusiasm in the sense of madness. In ridiculing a form of atheism as enthusiastic madness through the reductive system of the tailor-worshippers, he was simply adopting and turning to his own use a well-established convention of Anglican rationalist polemics against the atheists. By examining these polemics further, we can find an explanation for Swift's choice of materialism to represent irreligion and for his division of the tailor-worshippers into two branches.

In our attention to Anglican rationalist polemics against Catholics and Puritans, we ought not to forget that these divines devoted just as much attention to attacking the atheists. Cudworth, in fact, was concerned with them exclusively, and More gave them far more attention than he gave the Puritans, while Tillotson spent as much time preaching against the atheists as against the Catholics. Since atheism was one of the major issues of religious apologetics in that era, a young clergyman setting out to write a satire on abuses in religion would consider this threat to religion as important and necessary a target as either Catholicism or Puritanism. Religious polemics against atheism in the Restoration era generally attacked it under several forms. One of these was materialism.

Materialism, of course, by its very definition is an atheistic belief, for it rejects spiritual substance, and God is a spirit. At the same time, materialism denies the spirituality of the human soul, and it was on these grounds particularly that it was attacked, as the negation of all religion.

> By the soul [Tillotson wrote in his series of sermons on the immortality of the soul] we mean a part of man distinct from his body, or a principle in him which is not matter. . . . So that by the soul or spirit of a man, we mean some principle in man, which is really distinct from his visible and sensible part,

[32] *The True Intellectual System of the Universe* (London, 1678), p. 134.

from all that in man which affects our outward senses, and which is not to be described by any sensible and external qualities, such as we use to describe a body by: because it is supposed to be of such a nature, as does not fall under the cognizance and notice of any of our senses.[33]

But it was just those matters which do not "fall under the cognizance and notice of any of our senses" which were rejected by most materialists, "who," as one churchman complained, "because they believe nothing but what is palpable and visible, deny therefore *Spirits* and all *supernatural* effects; and consequently the truth of all relations, wherein *supernatural* causes are ingaged." [34]

There were some materialists, however, who, while rejecting spiritual substance and maintaining that whatever exists is material, nevertheless recognized the existence of the human soul, though not, of course, its spirituality. The most prominent materialist of this kind was Hobbes, who probably received more abuse from the pulpit than any other single figure during the Restoration era. He was, Tillotson declared in one of his sermons, "one, who hath done more by his writings to debauch the age with atheistical principles than any man that lives in it." [35] One of these "atheistical principles" which came under particularly heated attack was his doctrine that the soul itself is material. He declared in the *Leviathan* that "every part of the Universe, is Body, and that which is not Body, is no part of the Universe: And because the Universe is All, that which is no part of it, is *Nothing*; and consequently *no where*." But he did not thereby dismiss the existence of the human soul, for he went on to add: "Nor does it follow from hence, that Spirits are *nothing*, for they have dimensions, and are therefore really *Bodies*, though that name in common Speech be given to such Bodies onely, as are visible, or palpable; that is, that have some degree of Opacity." [36] Man, therefore, is an animal compounded of two corporeal substances, the soul and the body, and both these material parts, he taught, are mortal, and both are received from our parents *ex traduce.*

[33] *Works* (London, 1820), VII, 530.
[34] Casaubon, *Of Credulity and Incredulity, in Things Natural, Civil, and Divine* (London, 1668), p. 82.
[35] *Works*, I, 394.
[36] *Leviathan, or the Matter, Forme, & Power of a Common-Wealth Ecclesiasticall and Civill* (London, 1651), p. 371.

Materialism, whether it took the form of denying the soul by believing "nothing but what is palpable and visible" or of acknowledging the soul at the expense of its spirituality, was of course attacked as a threat to the very foundations of religion by Puritans and Anglicans alike. But the Anglican rationalists had at their disposal a particularly effective means of ridiculing the materialists in their convention of portraying atheists as enthusiastic madmen. One of the ways they adopted for discouraging the Anglican faithful from toying with materialism, therefore, was to concentrate on the severe limitations in accepting only the material side of existence and to ridicule the materialists as madmen who had put blinders on their understandings. "All *Atheists* are mere *Corporealists*," Cudworth wrote, "that is, acknowledge no other *Substance* besides *Body* or *Matter*." Consequently,

> the same Dull and Earthly Disbelief or confounded Sottishness of Mind, which makes men deny a *God*, must needs incline them to deny all *Incorporeal Substance* also. Wherefore as the Physicians speak of a certain *Disease* or *Madness*, called *Hydrophobia, the Symptome of those that have been bitten by a mad Dog*, which makes them have a monstrous Antipathy to Water; so all Atheists are possessed with a certain kind of *Madness*, that may be called *Pneumatophobia*, that makes them have an irrational but desperate Abhorrence from *Spirits* or *Incorporeal Substances*, they being acted also, at the same time, with an *Hylomania*, whereby they *Madly dote* upon *Matter*, and *Devoutly worship* it, as the only *Numen*.[37]

Swift used this convention to good effect in Section II of *A Tale of a Tub*, where the reductive system of the tailor-worshippers leads them to "madly dote upon matter" in the shape of clothing, which they "devoutly worship" as the unique principle of the universe, every part of which, to their disordered understandings, exists in this material form. Under the influence of such a sect as this, it was the most natural thing in the world for the three brothers to forget their father's commands and to begin defacing their coats with alacrity.

Furthermore, the two branches of tailor-worshippers described by Swift correspond exactly to the two kinds of materialists. Those

[37] *True Intellectual System*, p. 135.

who, ignoring the soul altogether, simply considered man a suit of clothes, are, of course, the common variety of materialists who "believe nothing but what is palpable and visible" and disregard the soul. Their more ingenious colleagues who, "though agreeing in the main system, . . . held that man was an animal compounded of two dresses, the natural and the celestial suit, which were the body and the soul," are, of course, followers of Hobbes and recognize the soul as separate from the body though consisting of the same materials. They even rely for support of their theory upon certain philosophical formulas which were suspected at the time of lending support to the materialism of Hobbes. Because of this suspicion, both formulas — *"ex traduce"* and "All in All, and All in every Part" — had come under attack during the Restoration era. Traducianism was of course rejected as part of Hobbes's theory about the soul. So Glanvill, for example, derided "that *silly* conceit of the *Souls Traduction* . . . which either ariseth from *direct Sadducism*, or a *defect* in Philosophy. Hereby our *Immortality*," he remarked, "is undermined, and dangerously exposed."[38] The second formula, on the other hand, was in reality not materialistic at all, not at least as first formulated. "All in all, and all in every part" was, of course, a perfectly orthodox formula in reference to the soul used both by St. Augustine and by St. Thomas. But it was regarded with such disfavor by More and his friends in their common defense of the spirituality of the soul that Glanvill, detailing the characteristic beliefs of the Anglican rationalists, was able to state that they all agreed that "the Doctrine of the common Schools of *Tota in Toto* . . . was one great occasion of the *Sadducism*, and disbelief of *Spiritual Beings*, which was so much the Mode of that age."[39] For Swift's purposes, then, one formula was associated with materialism quite as much as the other, and both could serve equally well to identify the tailor-worshippers who repeated them as followers of Hobbes.

As the most prominent materialist of the day, Hobbes received further recognition by ridicule in Swift's description of the beliefs of the tailor-worshippers. In presenting the reductive system of the tailor-worshippers as an attempt to explain every part of the uni-

[38] *Philosophia Pia*, p. 28.
[39] "Anti-fanatical Religion," *Essays* (London, 1676), p. 53. For St. Augustine's use of the formula, see *De Trinitate*, bk. VI, chap. 6; for its use by St. Thomas, see *Summa*, I, 76, 8.

verse in reference to the principle of clothing, Swift offers an elaborate explanation whereby the mad sect justifies its curious belief. "Look on this Globe of Earth," he writes, "you will find it to be a very compleat and fashionable *Dress*." He continues:

> What is that which some call *Land*, but a fine Coat faced with Green ? or the Sea, but a Wastcoat of Water-Tabby ? Proceed to the particular Works of the Creation, you will find how curious *Journey-man* Nature hath been, to trim up the *vegetable* Beaux: Observe how sparkish a Perewig adorns the Head of a *Beech*, and what a fine Doublet of white Satin is worn by the *Birch*. To conclude from all, what is Man himself but a *Micro-Coat*, or rather a compleat Suit of Cloaths with all its Trimmings? As to his Body, there can be no dispute; but examine even the Acquirements of his Mind, you will find them all contribute in their Order, towards furnishing out an exact Dress: To instance no more; Is not Religion a *Cloak*, Honesty a *Pair of Shoes*, worn out in the Dirt, Self-love a *Surtout*, Vanity a *Shirt*, and Conscience a *Pair of Breeches* [I, 47].

This passage, I suggest, is a parody of the famous opening of Hobbes's *Leviathan*, which I think will become apparent if we compare the following passage from the first paragraph of Hobbes's book with that which I have just quoted from the account of the tailor-worshippers:

> For what is the *Heart*, but a *Spring*; and the *Nerves*, but so many *Strings*; and the *Joynts*, but so many *Wheeles*, giving motion to the whole Body, such as was intended by the Artificer? *Art* goes yet further, imitating that Rationall and most excellent worke of Nature, *Man*. For by Art is created that great LEVIATHAN called a COMMONWEALTH, or STATE, (in latine CIVITAS) which is but an Artificiall Man; though of greater stature and strength than the Naturall, for whose protection and defence it was intended; and in which the *Soveraignty* is an Artificiall *Soul*, as giving life and motion to the whole body; The *Magistrates*, and other *Officers* of Judicature and Execution, artificiall *Joynts*; *Reward* and *Punishment* (by which fastned to the seate of the Soveraignty, every joynt and member is moved to performe his duty) are the *Nerves*, that do the same in the Body Naturall; The *Wealth* and *Riches* of

all the particular members, are the *Strength*; *Salus Populi* (the *peoples safety*) its *Businesse*; *Counsellors*, by whom all things needfull for it to know, are suggested unto it, are the *Memory*; *Equity* and *Lawes*, an artificiall *Reason* and *Will*; *Concord, Health*; *Sedition, Sicknesse*; *and Civill war, Death*.[40]

When it was that Swift had read and annotated the marked copy of the *Leviathan* listed among his books in 1715, we do not know. But in "The Preface" to *A Tale of a Tub* he referred to "*Hobbes's Leviathan*, which tosses and plays with all other Schemes of Religion and Government" (I, 24), and it is hard to believe that at this time he had not read at least the opening paragraph of the most controversial book of the age. In this paragraph Hobbes is of course simply developing an elaborate analogy of part to part and whole to whole. But since he expresses this analogy as a series of metaphors rather than of similes, it was possible for Swift to present it as an equation in his parody, simply changing the terms, and thus to transform Hobbes's analogy into a ridiculous reductive system which was still close enough to the original to be recognizable. In this way the beliefs of the tailor-worshippers themselves could be expressed in terms reminiscent of those of their arch-leader, Hobbes.

Swift offers one other reductive system in *A Tale of a Tub*. This occurs in Section IX, the "Digression concerning Madness," where he presents the three

> greatest Actions that have been performed in the World, under the Influence of Single Men; which are, *The Establishment of New Empires by Conquest: The Advance and Progress of New Schemes in Philosophy; and the contriving, as well as the propagating of New Religions* [I, 102].

In every one of these actions, he adds, "we shall find the Authors of them all, to have been Persons, whose natural Reason hath admitted great Revolutions." In short, they have all been mad. The last of these great actions, "the contriving as well as the propagating of new religions," he does not discuss here because, as we have seen, he had just finished treating it under the form of Aeolism in the preceding section. Having established once and for all that religious fanaticism is enthusiastic madness, his pur-

[40] *Leviathan*, p. 1.

85

pose here is not to discuss this subject further but to show that the authors of the two other greatest actions share the same disorder with the founders of new religions.

Swift's description of "the establishment of new empires by conquest" need not detain us at this point. It does not pertain to a reductive system as such, and its function in Section IX will be discussed later. The idea of presenting military conquest as a form of madness was Swift's own contribution to the conventions we are considering, and the examples he offers of Henri IV and Louis XIV as madmen raise no difficulties for the reader. The same cannot be said of his description of "the advance and progress of new schemes in philosophy," however, which is neither entirely original nor immediately clear.

Swift begins his discussion of "the great Introducers of new Schemes in Philosophy" by declaring that

> it is plain, that several of the chief among them, both *Antient* and *Modern,* were usually mistaken by their Adversaries, and indeed, by all, except their own Followers, to have been Persons Crazed, or out of their Wits, having generally proceeded in the common Course of their Words and Actions, by a Method very different from the vulgar Dictates of *unrefined* Reason: agreeing for the most Part in their several Models, with their present undoubted Successors in the *Academy* of *Modern Bedlam* [I, 105].

He then proceeds to offer "proof" for this statement by citing examples of mad philosophers of this kind. He had already presented one "scheme in philosophy" as a form of enthusiastic madness, of course, in his sect of the tailor-worshippers. But this sect had been described seven sections before the "Digression concerning Madness," and at this point Swift needed fresh examples of mad schemes in philosophy. The new examples of "introducers" of such schemes whom he chooses to discuss are Epicurus and Descartes.

After he has suggested the similarity between some of the inventors of new schemes in philosophy, "both ancient and modern," and the inhabitants of Bedlam, Swift continues:

> Of this Kind were *Epicurus, Diogenes, Apollonius, Lucretius, Paracelsus, Des Cartes,* and others; who, if they were now in the World, tied fast, and separate from their Fol-

lowers, would in this our undistinguishing Age, incur manifest Danger of *Phlebotomy*, and *Whips*, and *Chains*, and *dark Chambers*, and *Straw* [I, 105].

The first four names on this list are drawn from antiquity, the last two from modern times, in keeping with Swift's earlier remark that madmen have been found among "both ancient and modern" philosophers. The implication is clear that madness in philosophy is not the peculiar property of any age. But if Swift's list is representative of both ancient and modern times, it certainly is not representative of all philosophers. The six philosophers he mentions fall into two groups. The two philosophers who are the actual subject of the whole discussion of "introducers of new schemes in philosophy" are obviously Epicurus and Descartes, whom Swift goes on to treat more fully a little later. Lucretius is simply included in this list as the popularizer of the Epicurean system. But the other group of philosophers whom Swift mentions were, in the minds of his readers at least, of an altogether different sort. Apollonius of Tyana and Paracelsus were two of the most prominent magical occultists of their respective eras, one ancient, the other modern.[41] Diogenes is not the famous Cynic philosopher, I suggest, who was by no stretch of the imagination the introducer of a new system in philosophy nor the follower of any system at all, but Diogenes Apollonites, whom Swift had seen mentioned as a disciple of Anaximenes on the same page of Stanley's *History of Philosophy* from which, in all probability, he had taken his account of the Aeolists' beliefs, and whom he may, for that matter, have confused with the more famous philosopher of that name.[42] This second group consists, then, of notorious examples of occultists and reductive philosophers such as Swift had already used earlier to epitomize philosophical enthusiasm. His method here is essentially the same as he had employed previously in describing the sect of the Aeolists. It is no more credible that he is bothering to satirize the magical occultists and the followers of Anaximenes in Section IX than that he was attempting to do so in Section VIII, and his reason for introducing such contemptible figures here is the same that led him to introduce them into

[41] It is worth recalling that, as I mentioned earlier in this chapter, Paracelsus is discussed at some length in *Enthusiasmus Triumphatus* as a typical philosophical enthusiast, or occultist.
[42] See Stanley, *History of Philosophy*, p. 62.

his account of the Aeolists. He satirizes Epicurus and Descartes by degrading them to the level of, and yoking them together with, philosophical enthusiasts, just as previously he had satirized the Puritans by identifying them with the same contemptible group. In closely associating Epicurus and Descartes with the philosophical enthusiasts, Swift suggests that these two great philosophers suffered from the same disorder as their less famous and infinitely less respectable colleagues.

Immediately after presenting this catalogue of mad philosophers in which he indiscriminately mingles the names of Epicurus and Descartes with those of notorious philosophical enthusiasts, Swift proceeds to explain why all of these philosophers were mad. In doing so, he focuses his attention on the actual targets of his satire, Epicurus and Descartes themselves:

> For, what Man in the natural State, or Course of Thinking, did ever conceive it in his Power, to reduce the Notions of all Mankind, exactly to the same Length, and Breadth, and Heighth of his own? Yet this is the first humble and civil Design of all Innovators in the Empire of Reason. *Epicurus* modestly hoped, that one Time or other, a certain Fortuitous Concourse of all Mens Opinions, after perpetual Justlings, the Sharp with the Smooth, the Light and the Heavy, the Round and the Square, would by certain *Clinamina,* unite in the Notions of *Atoms* and *Void,* as these did in the Originals of all Things. *Cartesius* reckoned to see before he died, the Sentiments of all Philosophers, like so many lesser Stars in his *Romantick* System, rapt and drawn within his own *Vortex* [I, 105].

We must consider, to begin with, why Swift chose to satirize these two philosophers, one ancient, the other modern, and in what respect if any their teachings find a place among "abuses in religion"; for it has been suggested in recent years that the teachings of these two philosophers are attacked in *A Tale of a Tub* for playing a significant part in the new philosophy and the new science espoused by the members of the Royal Society and that they find a place more properly, therefore, among "abuses in learning." [43]

[43] See Miriam K. Starkman, *Swift's Satire on Learning,* chaps. i, ii, and iii.

It is particularly noticeable that Swift is not satirizing the Epicurean and Cartesian philosophies in their entirety. He says nothing, for example, of the Epicurean theory of happiness, so much discussed at the time, nor does he say anything of Cartesian metaphysics, which received even more attention from his contemporaries. Swift limits his satire, on the contrary, to the theories of Epicurus and Descartes concerning the origin of the universe, as his concentration on the atoms of Epicurus and the vortices of Descartes makes clear. Now if we turn once more to the tradition of Anglican polemics against atheism, we shall find that these were directed quite as much against certain cosmologies which denied or limited the creation or continued support of the universe by God, as they were against materialism.

Three such cosmologies came under particular attack during the Restoration era. One of these was the Aristotelian hypothesis that the world is eternal. Since this eliminated the possibility of the Creation, it was of course attacked by the Anglican clergy. But as this hypothesis had not been revived to any important extent, those who attacked it were content simply to disprove it.

The second of these cosmologies, on the other hand, was violently abused in the sermons and discourses of the period. This was the atomology of Democritus, Leucippus, Epicurus, and Lucretius. The account which these "atheists, those whom I call the Epicureans, do give of the existence of the world" was described by Tillotson to his congregation as follows:

> They suppose the matter, of which the world is constituted, to be eternal and of itself, and then an infinite empty space for the infinite little parts of this matter (which they call atoms) to move and play in; and that these, being always in motion, did, after infinite trials and encounters, without any counsel or design, and without the disposal and contrivance of any wise and intelligent Being, at last by a lucky casualty entangle and settle themselves in this beautiful and regular frame of the world which we now see.[44]

This theory, Tillotson assured his listeners, is "ridiculous and against all reason" and advanced only by "shameful beggars of principles." In so describing the Epicurean cosmology, he was merely echoing the sentiments of his fellow divines. Stillingfleet

[44] *Works,* I, 345–46.

declared that to believe "that all these things came only from a blind and fortuitous concourse of *Atoms,* is the most prodigious piece of credulity and folly, that Human Nature is subject to," while Cudworth described the "Democritick *Hypothesis*" as "rather a Madness than a Philosophy." [45]

Such strong abuse reflects much more than an antiquarian interest in the errors of ancient paganism. For the "Democritick hypothesis" had been revived by Hobbes, and it was at Hobbes that the divines were actually striking through their abuse of Epicurus and his disciples. It was Epicurus of course whom they assailed by name in denouncing atomism. But this abuse of Epicurus was often followed by an oblique reference to Hobbes as "a Modern Atheistick Writer" or "a person that is not very fond of Religion." [46]

One wonders, naturally, whether in attacking Hobbes through Epicurus these divines were also attacking the Royal Society and implying that the "new philosophy" celebrated by that group was also a revival of Epicurean atomism. Nothing, however, could be further from the truth. In fact, the Anglican rationalists were either members or supporters of the Royal Society and of the "new philosophy." So closely were they associated with the aims of the Royal Society and of the new philosophy that Glanvill, in describing the group under the name of the "Divines of Bensalem," coupled their emphasis upon the importance of reason in religion with their equally characteristic emphasis upon the new philosophy and entitled his essay "Anti-fanatical Religion and Free Philosophy." [47]

In the preface to his *Enchiridion Metaphysicum,* which contained his strongest attacks upon the atomism of Epicurus and Hobbes, More was careful to distinguish between these promoters of atheism and the members of the Royal Society, between the

[45] Tillotson, *ibid.,* I, 348; Stillingfleet, *Origines Sacrae* (7th ed.; Cambridge, 1702), p. 313; Cudworth, *True Intellectual System,* p. 53.

[46] For a typical example of this practice, see Cudworth, *ibid.,* p. 634. For an excellent discussion of the reaction to the atomism of Epicurus and Hobbes, see Charles T. Harrison, "The Ancient Atomists and English Literature of the Seventeenth Century," *Harvard Studies in Classical Philology,* XLV (1934), 1–79.

[47] For a similar characterization of the group, see S. P., *A Brief Account of the New Sect of Latitude-Men together with Some Reflections upon the New Philosophy* (London, 1662).

mechanical philosophy of the former and the experimental philosophy of the latter. And he was as generous in his praise of the one as he was unstinting in his abuse of the other.[48] For Cudworth, the distinction lay between "two several *Forms* of *Atomical Philosophy*." The one was "the *Adulterated Atheistick Atomology*, called *Leucippean* or *Democritical*," that makes "*Sensless and Lifeless Atoms, to be the only Principles of all things in the Universe*, thereby necessarily excluding . . . a *Deity*." The other was "the most Ancient and *Genuine* that was Religious, called *Moschical* (or if you will *Mosaical*) and *Pythagorical*, . . . acknowledging besides *Extended Substance* and *Corporeal Atoms*, another *Cogitative Incorporeal Substance*, and joyning *Metaphysicks* or *Theology*, together with *Physiology*, to make up one entire *System of Philosophy*."[49] The former had been revived by Hobbes, while the latter was that of the Royal Society. Glanvill makes a similar distinction, although again the terms are different. On the one hand, he distinguishes the "Mechanick Atheists," "men of the *Epicurean* sort," and "*those* of Mr. *Hobb's* way," who hold "the opinion of the *world's* being made by a *fortuitous jumble* of *Atoms*," which Glanvill condemns as "the most *unphilosophical* phansie, and *ridiculous* dotage in the world." Opposed to these, however, are "the late Restorers of the *Corpuscularian Hypothesis*," that is, the members of the Royal Society, who "suppose, and teach, *That God created matter, and is the supreme Orderer of its motions, by which all those diversities are made*."[50]

This was of course a distinction which the empiricists themselves were constantly making. Robert Boyle, for instance, was anxious to dissociate himself and his colleagues in the Royal Society, men who professed "the acknowledgment and adoration of

[48] "*Haec autem omnia ita intelligi velim, ut Experimentalis Philosophiae, quam quidam imperite cum Mechanica confundunt, pretium & existimatio nullatenus minuatur; qualem nempe celeberrima* Regia Societas Londinensis *profitetur, & in quo genere multa ac praeclara edidit Artis industriaeque suae Specimina, non solum ad communes Vitae usus, sed, quod & praesens hoc* Enchiridion *testari potest, ad Veritates Philosophicas maxime sublimes vereque Metaphysicas eruendas, apprime utilia*" (*Enchiridion Metaphysicum* [London, 1671], sig. B2).
[49] *True Intellectual System*, pp. 174–75.
[50] *Philosophia Pia*, pp. 106–9.

a most Intelligent, Powerful and Benign Author of things," from those atheistic atomists who "ascribe such admirable Effects to so incompetent and pitiful a Cause as Blind Chance, or the tumultuous Justlings of Atomical Portions of senseless Matter." [51] Samuel Parker and John Ray, two of the most prominent apologists for the Royal Society during the Restoration era, attacked the cosmology of Epicurus in much the same way as did the Anglican rationalists.[52] The new philosophy broached by the Royal Society, therefore, was in no danger of being associated with the atheism of Epicurus.

The third cosmology which was particularly attacked by the Anglican clergy of the Restoration era was that of Descartes. The account which he gave of the origin of the world, as Cudworth described it,

> makes God to contribute nothing more to the Fabrick of the World, than the Turning round of a *Vortex* or Whirlpool of Matter; from the fortuitous Motion of which, according to certain General Laws of Nature, must proceed all this Frame of things that now is, the exact Organization, and successive Generation of Animals, without the Guidance of any Mind or Wisdom.[53]

Such a cosmology was not atheistic, since it acknowledged that God first set the vortex in motion, but it denied Providence and resulted in "the banishing of all *Final* and *Mental Causality* quite out of the World," by which, Cudworth pointed out, Descartes had outdone "even the very Atheists themselves." [54] Similarly, More pronounced the Cartesian cosmology a piece of "eminent folly," for it "leads from God, or obstructs the way to him, by prescinding all pretence of finding his Footsteps in the works of the Creation, excluding the *Final cause* of things, and making us believe that all comes to pass by a blinde, but necessary, Jumble of the Matter." [55]

Here again the Anglican rationalists were simply reflecting an

[51] *The Christian Virtuoso* (London, 1690), p. 9.
[52] See Parker, *Disputationes de Deo et Providentia Divina* (London, 1678), pp. 221–351; Ray, *The Wisdom of God Manifested in the Works of the Creation* (2nd ed.; London, 1692), pp. 13–28.
[53] *True Intellectual System*, p. 54.
[54] *Ibid.*, p. 175.
[55] *Divine Dialogues* (London, 1668),I, 47–48.

attitude shared by their fellow members and supporters of the Royal Society, the "physico-theologians." Although some apologists for the Royal Society favored Descartes' metaphysics, their hostility to his cosmology was notorious. They attacked his explanation for the origin of the universe quite as often as they did that of Epicurus, and, in view of Swift's coupling of the two philosophers, it is interesting to notice that they often joined them together in the same way. The third of Samuel Parker's *Disputationes de Deo et Providentia Divina* is entitled "Epicuri & Cartesii Hypotheses de rerum Fabricatione evertuntur." John Ray, Cudworth, Stillingfleet, and More all employ the same combination of Epicurus and Descartes, sometimes adding the Aristotelian hypothesis of the eternity of the world and sometimes omitting it.[56]

As we noticed of their attacks on materialism, the Anglican rationalists, in denouncing the Epicurean and Cartesian explanations for the origin of the universe, shared these targets with many other divines of their age, particularly the "physico-theologians," but employed a method which was largely their own. For ridiculing Epicurus and Descartes, as well as materialism, they could make use of their convention of treating atheists and their supporters as enthusiastic madmen. It was More, as we might expect, who used this convention to best effect in ridiculing the cosmology of Descartes, and for once he abandoned description for dramatization. In his *Divine Dialogues* (1668), a series of Socratic dialogues on various religious and philosophical subjects, More introduces several dramatic characters, representing different intellectual positions, who are invariably bested in argument by another character, "Philotheus," who represents More himself.[57] One of the subjects discussed in these dialogues is Descartes' theory

[56] See Parker, *Disputationes*, pp. 221–351; Ray, *The Wisdom of God*, pp. 13–28; Cudworth, *True Intellectual System*, pp. 53–54, 174–75; Stillingfleet, *Origines Sacrae*, pp. 301–16; More, *Enchiridion Metaphysicum, passim*. For studies of the reaction to Descartes, see Marjorie Nicolson, "The Early Stage of Cartesianism in England," *Studies in Philology*, XXVI (1929), 356–74; Sterling P. Lamprecht, "The Role of Descartes in Seventeenth-Century England," *Studies in the History of Ideas,* III (New York, 1935), 181–240.

[57] For a persuasive argument that Philotheus represents More and not, as is sometimes suggested, Cudworth, see J. A. Passmore, *Ralph Cudworth: An Interpretation* (Cambridge, 1951), pp. 17–18.

of the origin of the universe, which "Philotheus" demolishes to the satisfaction of most of his listeners. The character who speaks on behalf of the Cartesian cosmology is a young man named "Cuphophron," who, as an enthusiast of sorts, launches into philosophical raptures from time to time throughout the dialogues to the amusement of the other characters. More describes Cuphophron in his preface as "a zealous, but Airie-minded, *Platonist* and *Cartesian,* or *Mechanist.*" [58] He is a "Platonist," of course, only in the sense that Thomas Vaughan was one. And lest anyone suspect the Cambridge Platonist of self-criticism, More points out

> *that the Character of* Cuphophron *is not simply* a Platonist, *but an* aiery-minded one, (*as indeed both the danger and* indecorum *of Light-mindedness or over-much Levity of spirit is both represented and perstringed all along in his person*;) *which therefore does not redound to the discredit of* Platonism *as such.*[59]

In the dialogues which follow, Cuphophron frequently indulges in wild metaphysical flights of fancy which betray a strong penchant for the occult. "*Metaphysicks* were not *Metaphysicks, Hylobares,* if they were not mysterious," he remarks at one point to one of his friends.[60] But, at the same time, Cuphophron is as enthusiastic in his admiration for Descartes as in his love for the occult. It is for his physical theories, such as his explanation for the origin of the universe, that Cuphophron admires the French philosopher. From time to time he enlivens the dialogues with extravagant eulogies of "that stupendious Wit *Des-Cartes*" and at one point disarmingly admits to a friend: "I must confess, O *Philopolis,* there is an extraordinary and peculiar congruity of spirit betwixt me and *Des-Cartes.*" [61]

This, then, is the background of Swift's discussion of the "introducers of new schemes in philosophy" and his satire of Epicurus and Descartes in *A Tale of a Tub.* In ridiculing these two philosophers for their theories concerning the origin of the universe by portraying them as mad enthusiasts, he was simply attacking another of the notorious "abuses in religion" condemned by most

[58] *Divine Dialogues*, I, sig. b4v.
[59] *Ibid.*, I, sig. a4.
[60] *Ibid.*, I, 150.
[61] *Ibid.*, I, 52, 120.

churchmen of his day and turning to his own use once more a convention of Anglican rationalist apologetics which he had found particularly apt elsewhere in his religious satire. In doing so, he was no more reflecting on all philosophers nor making unfounded accusations against the "new philosophy" than were his fellow clergymen who made use of the same convention for ridiculing the same targets.

Let us turn now to a consideration of how Swift satirizes the theories of Epicurus and Descartes concerning the origin of the universe and of the artistic use to which he puts the homiletic conventions of attack which we have been examining. Swift's specific intention is the same as that of the Anglican rationalists whose polemics I have been quoting: to ridicule the "irreligious" theories of Epicurus and Descartes concerning the origin of the universe by presenting them as the beliefs of madmen. But whereas Swift's predecessors had been content to label these theories themselves as mad, Swift substitutes ridicule for invective by using these theories as evidence in support of a general thesis as to what constitutes a mad philosopher. In this way a comic "proof" that Epicurus and Descartes were madmen replaces the mere assertion that this was the case. Swift asks: "For, what Man in the natural State, or Course of Thinking, did ever conceive it in his Power, to reduce the Notions of all Mankind, exactly to the same Length, and Breadth, and Heighth of his own?" Assuming a negative answer to his question, he proceeds to offer a general thesis applicable to all mad philosophers: "Yet this is the first humble and civil Design of all Innovators in the Empire of Reason." Madness among such philosophers, then, consists in the hope of converting all mankind to one's peculiar philosophical beliefs, that is, in the attempt to make proselytes. The examples which Swift proceeds to offer the reader serve both to illustrate this thesis and at the same time — provided one accepts the thesis — to prove Epicurus and Descartes madmen.

> *Epicurus* [he writes] modestly hoped, that one Time or other, a certain Fortuitous Concourse of all Mens Opinions, after perpetual Justlings, the Sharp with the Smooth, the Light and the Heavy, the Round and the Square, would by certain *Clinamina*, unite in the Notions of *Atoms* and *Void*, as these did in the Originals of all Things.

95

Turning to Descartes, he continues: "*Cartesius* reckoned to see before he died, the Sentiments of all Philosophers, like so many lesser Stars in his *Romantick* System, rapt and drawn within his own *Vortex*."

These philosophers — Epicurus, Descartes, and the magical occultists named with them — were mad, Swift suggests, because they were all inventors of reductive systems who hoped against all reason to reduce the complexity of human thought to some simple formula in the same way that they reduced the complex phenomena of existence to a simple principle of explanation. They were reductive then in a double sense, as the amusing account of the hopes of Epicurus and Descartes in terms of their own systems illustrates. They were reductive philosophers in one sense, of course, because, like the Aeolists and tailor-worshippers described earlier, they were designers or propagators of monistic systems of thought. But they were reductive philosophers also in the sense that they hoped to convert the world to their way of thinking by striving "to reduce the notions of all mankind" to the simple formula they offered through their systems. Zeal is equally noticeable in both their efforts, for Epicurus and Descartes, as Swift pictures them, were quite as eager to reduce other men's opinions to their own as they were to reduce the complex origin and operations of the universe to the single principle of atoms or vortices.

In their fervor "to advance new Systems with such an eager Zeal" and to make proselytes of all mankind, these philosophers are not essentially different from the religious fanatics. Both groups are bent upon winning converts, and the only noticeable difference between them is that the fanatics wish to proselytize mankind to their novel religious beliefs, whereas the "atheistic" philosophers wish to persuade all men to adopt their irreligious opinions. Both groups, in short, provide instances of what Henry More had described in *Enthusiasmus Triumphatus* as "political enthusiasm." More himself had presented the religious fanaticism of the sects as a prime example of political enthusiasm because of the undeniable political repercussions to which the public activities of the fanatics had given rise both in England and abroad. But, while the notion of atheism as another form of enthusiasm was borrowed, as we have seen, from More and his imitators, the idea of presenting atheism as another form of political enthusiasm was Swift's own invention. In his picture of Epicurus and Descartes, these two "atheistic" cosmologists emerge unmistakably as zealots, proselytizers, and disturbers of the commonwealth whose method of propagating their opinions and winning converts is not noticeably different from that of John of Leyden or David George.

It is not only "the contriving, as well as the propagating of new religions" which resembles "the advance and progress of new schemes in philosophy." Both of these activities are presented as essentially similar to the third of "the greatest actions that have been performed in the world, under the influence of single men": "the establishment of new empires by conquest." For the "innovators in the empire of reason" and the founders and propagators of new religions are described as being quite as eager to gain an influence over other men's minds as are conquerors to gain possession of their persons and property. All of "those mighty Revolutions, that have happened in *Empire*, in *Philosophy*, and in *Religion*," as Swift refers to these various activities a little later, have been struggles for power of one kind or another. Every one of these "single men" has had as his chief concern the intention of "subduing Multitudes to his own *Power,* his *Reasons* or his *Visions*" (I, 108). Once we perceive this, the function of the description of military conquerors in Section IX becomes clear. Swift is not suddenly and unaccountably digressing to satirize, for the first and only time in *A Tale of a Tub*, military conquests in general or French political ambitions in particular. His discussion of military conquerors as a third class of madmen is introduced at this point, not as an additional satirical target, but as a highly effective instrument of his religious satire which reinforces his characterization of both fanaticism and atheism as instances of the phenomenon described by More as "political enthusiasm." In this respect, Swift's introduction of Henri IV and Louis XIV is analogous to his introduction of Diogenes, Apollonius, and Paracelsus a little later. Both serve to degrade the character of novel religious and irreligious beliefs and the motives of their proponents.

While he does not fail to ridicule the "atheistic" theories of Epicurus and Descartes concerning the origin of the universe, then, as had his predecessors, Swift treats with even greater scorn their attempts to propagate these theories. The theories themselves are presented as absurd, being reductive systems, but the madness of their authors is attributed to their hopes of imposing these absurd beliefs upon the rest of mankind. What is true of Swift's picture of the "atheistic" cosmologists is equally true of his description of the religious fanatics. This emphasis is in keeping with the homiletic tradition on which Swift was drawing, besides reflecting a belief of his own which he was fond of repeating.

I have referred earlier in this chapter to the primary concern of the Anglican apologists in their anti-Puritan polemics with preventing further defections into dissent on the part of the Anglican faithful rather than with attempting to dissuade the dissenters themselves from their privately held beliefs. It is hardly surprising, therefore, that the zeal which they condemned in the Puritans was not so much the intensity of their private convictions as the passionate fervor with which they attempted to win proselytes. The tragic history of the Civil War and the Commonwealth, indeed, offered sufficient proof of the dangers to which such unrestrained zeal could lead. When in *Enthusiasmus Triumphatus* More characterized religious fanaticism as "political enthusiasm," he was simply emphasizing the social and political consequences that inevitably appear when founders of new religions arise, inspired by

> *Enthusiasm*, that puffs up men into an opinion that they have a more then ordinary influence from God that acts upon their Spirits, and that he designes them by special appointment to be *new Prophets, new Lawgivers, new Davids, new Messiases*, and what not? when it is nothing but the working of the *Old man* in them in a fanatical manner.[62]

Prophets must find followers who will accept their prophecies, lawgivers subjects to whom they can give laws; hence proselytizing always follows close upon inspiration, and social and political disturbances accompany the making of proselytes. More, writing in 1656, while Cromwell was yet alive and the Commonwealth still flourishing, could make no allusion to matters at home. But his references to the factions and turmoils caused by David George and other religious leaders on the Continent were intended as thinly disguised parallels to contemporary conditions in his own country.

[62] *Enthusiasmus Triumphatus*, p. 38.

In his sermons Swift employs the same emphasis in attacking the dissenters of his own day. He remarks, for example, in his "Sermon upon the Martyrdom of King Charles I":

> If [a dissenter's] religion be different from that of his country, and the government think fit to tolerate it, (which he may be very secure of, let it be what it will) he ought to be fully satisfied, and give no offence, by writing or discourse, to the worship established, as the dissenting preachers are too apt to do. But, if he hath any new visions of his own, it is his duty to be quiet, and possess them in silence, without disturbing the community by a furious zeal for making proselytes. This was the folly and madness of those antient Puritan fanatics: They must needs overturn heaven and earth, violate all the laws of God and man, make their country a field of blood, to propagate whatever wild or wicked opinions came into their heads, declaring all their absurdities and blasphemies to proceed from the Holy Ghost [IX, 227].[63]

A similar emphasis is noticeable where atheism appears as the subject of Anglican apologetics or of Swift's sermons and other writings on religion. Atheistic theories are of course themselves attacked and disproved in numerous Anglican sermons and discourses. But argument gives place to abuse whenever the preacher passes from his refutation of atheistic theories to a mention of prominent atheists. The attack centers not so much on the fact that these philosophers have held personally the unreasonable doctrines under discussion as on their having attempted to spread them. One need only recall in this connection the previously cited reference by Tillotson to Hobbes as "one, who hath done more by his writings to debauch the age with atheistical principles than any man that lives in it." [64] To permit such persons to promote disbelief is to endanger the peace, Tillotson argued, for "all the privilege that atheism pretends to is to let men loose to vice, which is naturally attended with temporal inconveniences." [65] Similarly, in his sermon "On the Testimony of Conscience," Swift writes that "it is certain, that Men who profess to have no Religion, are full as zealous to bring over Proselytes as any Papist or Fanatick can

[63] See also *Prose Works*, IX, 151, 261–63.
[64] *Works*, I, 394.
[65] *Ibid.*, I, 398.

be" (IX, 157). The danger of permitting such proselytizing on the part of the atheists is of the same kind and degree as was that of allowing the Puritans to make converts during the reign of Charles I. "The consequences of atheistical opinions published to the world," Swift writes in "Some Thoughts on Free-Thinking," "are not so immediate or so sensible, as doctrines of rebellion and sedition, spread in a proper season: However, I cannot but think the same consequences are as natural and probable for the former, though more remote" (IV, 50).

The rejection of reason, then, where religion is concerned, can lead, in the view of Swift and the Anglican rationalists, in either of two directions. It can lead to religious fanaticism, on the one hand, or to atheism on the other. In either event, the result is enthusiasm. And enthusiasm in either guise is inevitably accompanied by a "zeal for the cause" which drives its victim toward the winning of proselytes. To describe such a zealot as a madman, they felt, was no exaggeration, as had been proven true all too often by the consequences of such attempts. For as Swift remarks in one of his sermons, "Where the vulgar are deluded by false preachers, to grow fond of new visions and fancies in religion," the zeal of their leaders has "often made whole nations run mad" (IX, 229).

Chapter 4

REASON AND IMAGINATION

I have pointed out that in Section IX of *A Tale of a Tub*, the "Digression concerning Madness," Swift portrays enthusiasts as madmen, suggests that they may appear in the role of either religious fanatics or atheistic philosophers, and likens their zeal for making proselytes to the military ambitions of mad conquerors. What is still wanting is an explanation for the mad behavior of enthusiasts. In providing the answer to this question in the same section of his book, Swift offers an analysis of human aberration which for sheer power and sustained brilliance is scarcely to be equalled anywhere else in his writings. Not the least brilliant feature of this analysis is the number and variety of the causes which he suggests to account for enthusiastic madness and for the success of its victims in gaining disciples.

The first of these causes which Swift brings forward is physiological. Throughout the early part of Section IX, in which Swift presents the three "greatest Actions that have been performed in the World, under the Influence of Single Men; which are, *The Establishment of New Empires by Conquest: The Advance and Progress of New Schemes in Philosophy; and the contriving, as well as the propagating of New Religions*," he repeatedly describes the authors of these actions as victims of a physical disturbance which is responsible for their mental disorder. In the opening paragraph of the section he writes of these "greatest actions":

> We shall find the Authors of them all, to have been Persons, whose natural Reason hath admitted great Revolutions from their Dyet, their Education, the Prevalency of some certain

Temper, together with the particular Influence of Air and Climate. Besides, there is something Individual in human Minds, that easily kindles at the accidental Approach and Collision of certain Circumstances, which tho' of paltry and mean Appearance, do often flame out into the greatest Emergencies of Life. For great Turns are not always given by strong Hands, but by lucky Adaption, and at proper Seasons; and it is of no import, where the Fire was kindled, if the Vapor has once got up into the Brain. For the *upper Region* of Man, is furnished like the *middle Region* of the Air; The Materials are formed from Causes of the widest Difference, yet produce at last the same Substance and Effect. Mists arise from the Earth, Steams from Dunghils, Exhalations from the Sea, and Smoak from Fire; yet all Clouds are the same in Composition, as well as Consequences: and the Fumes issuing from a Jakes, will furnish as comely and useful a Vapor, as Incense from an Altar. Thus far, I suppose, will easily be granted me; and then it will follow, that as the Face of Nature never produces Rain, but when it is overcast and disturbed, so Human Understanding, seated in the Brain, must be troubled and overspread by Vapours, ascending from the lower Faculties, to water the Invention, and render it fruitful. Now, altho' these Vapours (as it hath been already said) are of as various Original, as those of the Skies, yet the Crop they produce, differs both in Kind and Degree, meerly according to the Soil [I, 102-3].

The lengthy discussion of conquerors, "introducers of new schemes in philosophy," and founders of new religions which follows is offered purportedly as an elaborate series of examples illustrating the thesis which concludes the above passage, that the madness which vapors create, or "Crop they produce, differs both in Kind and Degree, meerly according to the Soil," or Brain, of the particular madman. The "Projects and Preparations" for con quest of Henri IV and the actual triumphs on the battlefield which Louis XIV enjoyed "for the space of above thirty Years" are in either case shown to have been caused by a "*Vapour* or *Spirit*, which animated the Hero's Brain." Again, having described the hopes of Epicurus and Descartes for making proselytes of all mankind, Swift concludes:

Now, I would gladly be informed, how it is possible to account for such Imaginations as these in particular Men, without Recourse to my *Phaenomenon* of *Vapours*, ascending from the lower Faculties to over-shadow the Brain, and thence distilling into Conceptions, for which the Narrowness of our Mother-Tongue has not yet assigned any other Name, besides that of *Madness* or *Phrenzy* [I, 105].

Finally, when Swift takes up in turn the founders of new religions after concluding his discussion of mad philosophers, he remarks:

Of such great Emolument, is a Tincture of this *Vapour*, which the World calls *Madness*, that without its Help, the World would not only be deprived of those two great Blessings, *Conquests* and *Systems*, but even all Mankind would unhappily be reduced to the same Belief in Things Invisible [I, 107].

This portion of Section IX concludes with a comic attempt to account for the fact, now amply illustrated, "that it is of no Import from what Originals this *Vapour* proceeds, but either in what *Angles* it strikes and spreads over the Understanding, or upon what *Species* of Brain it ascends." The explanation, however, of "how this numerical Difference in the Brain, can produce Effects of so vast a Difference from the same *Vapour*, as to be the sole Point of Individuation between *Alexander the Great, Jack of Leyden*, and Monsieur *Des Cartes*" is never provided, due to a "*Defect in the Manuscript.*"

A satisfactory explanation for Swift's incessant preoccupation with vapors as the cause of madness in this part of the "Digression concerning Madness" must account for both his repeated statements that madness is caused by vapors and his choice of this particular theory as a peculiarly appropriate means of satirizing enthusiasm as madness. Such an explanation, as it happens, is readily available in More's *Enthusiasmus Triumphatus*, from which Swift seems to have borrowed his theory. For the vapors to which Swift attributes the madness of various leaders were the commonly recognized cause of a specific mental disorder which he nowhere actually names in Section IX. In *Enthusiasmus Triumphatus*, however, where these causes are discussed, the disorder itself which vapors produce is mentioned as well.

I pointed out in the last chapter that when, in 1656, More wrote his discourse on enthusiasm he took up the thesis, already put forward by Casaubon the previous year, that there is a natural explanation for enthusiasm and developed it further by finding this explanation in madness. I have been using the term "madness" in a loose sense to describe any form of mental disorder, and as a hyperbole for enthusiasm this term is by no means uncommon in the writings of More and his friends, as when Glanvill, speaking of the founders of the Puritan sects, declares that "he that can be the *Author* of a *new* kind of *madness*, shall *lead a Party*." [1] But where More and those who came after him choose their words more carefully, they speak of the enthusiasts as suffering from a dotage, as when More, writing of the fanatics' belief that they are supernaturally inspired, declares that "this certainly in them is as true, but farre worse, dotage, then to fancy a mans self either a *Cock* or *Bull*, when it is plain to the senses of all that he is a *Man*." [2] Both the fanatics and the man who believes himself a cock or bull, then, suffer from dotage, or mental disorder, but the latter, who is presumably in Bedlam, suffers from a different species of dotage than do the fanatics. The fact that the fanatics, while suffering from dotage, were clearly not eligible for Bedlam required an explanation which More and his friends were ready to offer. If the enthusiast was not to be found in Bedlam, this was not due to any laxity on the part of the authorities but to the fact that there was an important difference between the mental disorder of an ordinary lunatic and that of an enthusiast. Whereas the lunatic was completely out of his wits, behaving at all times and in all places in such a manner as to leave no doubt as to his disorder, the enthusiast was only irrational on one subject, in other respects behaving in a reasonable manner.

THAT which is most observable & most usefull for the present matter in hand [More observes early in his discourse] is, That notwithstanding there is such an enormous lapse of the Phansy and Judgement in some *one* thing, yet the party should be of sound mind in *all other*, according to his naturall capacities and abilities; which all Physicians acknowledge to be true, and are ready to make good by innumerable Examples.[3]

---

[1] *Philosophia Pia* (London, 1671), p. 224.
[2] "Enthusiasmus Triumphatus," *A Collection of Several Philosophical Writings of Dr. Henry More* (2d ed., London, 1662), p. 10.
[3] *Ibid.*, p. 9.

This peculiarity of the enthusiast's disorder, "that it may onely befool the Understanding in some one point, and leave it sound in the rest,"[4] accounts for the fact that it is not popularly recognized as true dotage. That the enthusiast should be normal in all respects save one was, More reasoned, an idea which it should not be difficult to grasp:

> Nor is it any more wonder that his Intellectuals should be sound in other things, though he be thus delirious in some one point, no more then that he that thinks he sees the devil in a wood, should not be at all mistaken in the circumstance of place, but see the very same path, flowers and grasse that another in his wits sees there as well as himself.[5]

In the tradition which we have seen that More established among his friends and followers for picturing the enthusiasts as mad, this distinction between the fanatics and other madmen persisted, and even Glanvill, who could refer to the Puritans at times as "fit for Bedlam," testified to the fact

> *That there is a sort of madness, which takes men in some particular things, when they are sound in others*: which one Proposition will afford a good account of many of the *Phaenomena* of *Enthusiasm*; and shews that the *extravagants* among us may be really *distracted* in the *affairs* of *Religion*, though their brains are untouch't in *other* matters.[6]

In order to make good this distinction between lunacy and enthusiasm while at the same time insisting that both were forms of mental disorder, More attributed the distraction of the fanatics to melancholy, which was commonly believed to include the peculiarity which distinguished the Puritans from lunatics. In his discussion of melancholy, More drew upon numerous medical treatises. But since he was particularly indebted, as his references confirm, to Robert Burton's *Anatomy of Melancholy* and since Swift seems, as we shall see, to share this indebtedness, it will be sufficient to explain More's emphasis upon melancholy by reference to Burton.

Dotage, as Burton explained, was simply the name for any form

[4] *Ibid.*, p. 28.
[5] *Ibid.*, p. 5.
[6] *Philosophia Pia*, pp. 63–64.

of mental disorder and comprehended several distinct species. The three principal species of dotage were madness, frenzy, and melancholy. Madness was that violent species of dotage associated with Bedlam, and frenzy a similar disorder, but accompanied by a fever.

> *Madness* [Burton writes] is therefore defined to be a vehement *dotage*, or raving without a fever, far more violent than *melancholy*, full of anger and clamour, horrible looks, actions, gestures, troubling the patients with far greater vehemency both of body and mind, without all fear and sorrow, with such impetuous force & boldness, that sometimes three or four men cannot hold them. Differing only in this from *phrenzy*, that it is without a fever, and their memory is most part better.[7]

Melancholy was a less violent dotage and betrayed its victims into madness on only one subject, so that they escaped the penalties of Bedlam. When this subject was religion, the result was enthusiasm, as Burton and numerous other students of melancholy took note. "Of these men," Burton wrote of the religious fanatics:

> I may conclude generally, that howsoever they may seem to be discreet, and men of understanding in other matters . . . they are like comets, round in all places but only where they blaze, . . . they have impregnable wits many of them, and discreet otherwise, but in this their madness and folly breaks out beyond measure [III, 4, 1, 3].

Burton, however, while agreeing with his numerous sources that enthusiasm was a form of melancholy, was at as great a loss as his predecessors as to how to classify or account for it. "No Physician," he explained, "hath as yet distinctly written of it, . . . all acknowledge it a most notable symptom, some a cause, but few a species or kind" (III, 4, 1, 1). Consequently, he placed it toward the end of his book, including it under "love melancholy," which was itself classified as an "indefinite kind of melancholy," though he conceded that "whether this subdivision of *Religious Melancholy* be warrantable, it may be controverted." He avoided, like-

[7] *The Anatomy of Melancholy*, ed. A. R. Shilleto (London, 1926), I, 160 [I, 1, 1, 4]. The standard system of reference to Burton, such as I have included here in brackets, will be used hereafter for the reader's convenience and will appear in the text.

wise, assigning any specific causes to the disorder and was content to attribute it to "the Devil, his instruments, and his engines."

When More came to write *Enthusiasmus Triumphatus*, then, and decided to picture the enthusiasts as victims of melancholy, he found at his disposal a fairly vague tradition, mostly confined to medical treatises, of classifying enthusiasm as religious melancholy. Casaubon, too, in his *Treatise concerning Enthusiasme* of the preceding year, had shown that he was aware of this tradition when he referred to his subject as a species of melancholy, but, like the medical writers to whom he referred, he had avoided the problem of its specific cause. What More needed, however, was a more specific account of the nature and cause of religious melancholy which would serve as a means of disparaging the enthusiasts. He provided such an account himself, assigning a specific physiological cause to enthusiasm, as well as a place among the recognized kinds of melancholy. In order to do this, he did not have to go beyond the analysis of melancholy already mapped out by Burton. All More had to do was to turn for the details of his discussion, not to the vague account of religious melancholy which appears toward the end of Burton's book, but to the clinical discussion of the causes and kinds of melancholy which Burton provides early in *The Anatomy of Melancholy*.

According to Burton, the immediate, physiological cause of melancholy depends upon the prevalence and condition of the victim's humors. Melancholy may result from a mere abundance of "natural melancholy," that is, one of the four humors which exist in all men. These humors, which are natural ingredients of the body, are four in number: sanguine, phlegm, choler, and melancholy. That melancholic condition which arises from an excess of natural melancholy, however, is a mild form of disorder, quite different from the ravings usually associated with enthusiasm. Such frenzies, Burton points out, "may be true in non-natural Melancholy, which produceth madness, but not in that natural, which is more cold, and, being immoderate, produceth a gentle dotage" (I, 2, 5, 2).

Unnatural melancholy was a term used to describe a dotage arising from an unnatural condition in any of the four humors. In its natural state "a humour is a liquid or fluent part of the body, comprehended in it, for the preservation of it" (I, 1, 2, 2,). In an unnatural state, however, a humor can assume an entirely different form. "Adventitious, peccant, or diseased humours," as Burton calls them, lose their liquid form, grow heated and become adust, and in the form of vapors rise to the brain to create disorder there by overclouding the judgment. Sanguine adust, choler adust, phlegm adust, melancholy adust, or any combination of adust or heated humors were equally designated by the general name of unnatural melancholy, or simply "melancholy," although each resulted in different symptoms. For, Burton pointed out, "these symptoms vary according to the mixture of those four humours adust, which is unnatural melancholy" (I, 3, 1, 3,). Whatever the combination of symptoms, however, and whatever the heated or adust humor that gave rise to them, one symptom was invariable. "Unnatural" melancholy was accompanied regularly by *vapours which arise from the other parts, and fume up into the head, altering the animal faculties* (I, 2, 5, 2).

Depending upon which of these "other parts" of the body the vapors originate in, melancholy can be classified according to three kinds, Burton explains.

> The first proceeds from the sole fault of the *brain*, & is called *head melancholy*: the second sympathetically proceeds from the *whole body*, when the whole temperature is melancholy: the third ariseth from the bowels, liver, spleen, or membrane called *mesenterium*, named *hypochondriacal or windy melancholy* [I, 1, 3, 4].

In all three kinds of melancholy, any humor or combination of humors may become adust, and in all three kinds the heated humors will find their way in the form of vapors to the brain. But, depending upon which of the three kinds of melancholy the victim suffers from, these vapors will have originated in the head itself, in the whole body, or in the lower region of the body alone.

Burton specifically had exempted "love melancholy" with its subspecies of religious melancholy from this classification as well as from his discussion of causes and symptoms, since they were but "an indefinite kind of melancholy." This was no matter to More. His purpose was to provide as degrading a "natural explanation" as possible for the supernatural inspiration to which the enthusiasts laid claim. If the medical treatises on melancholy which he consulted failed to provide him with the explanation he required, he could make good the omission himself by a judicious rearrangement of the materials with which they had provided him. Physicians might protest if they would, but enthusiasm was to be assigned the most ridiculous classification and the most contemptible cause in the entire catalogue of melancholic diseases.

With this end in view, More makes clear from the beginning of his discourse that enthusiasts are sufferers from "*Melancholy* when it reaches to a disease," that is to say, from "unnatural" melancholy in which one or the other of the victim's humors has grown heated and become adust. Since this is the enthusiast's plight, his head must be filled with vapors into which the heated humor has been converted, for "in these distempers we may well conclude that such fumes or vapours arise into the Brain from some foulnesse in the Body." [8] More proceeds to suggest that the humor which most often becomes adust in the enthusiast is natural melancholy. "Now no Complexion [humor] is so *hot* as *Melancholy* when it is *heated*, being like boiling water . . . so that it transcends the flame of fire; or it is like heated stone or iron when they are red hot, for they are then more hot by far then a burning Coal." [9] This is why the enthusiast is the most rabid of all melancholists, for

> assuredly *Melancholy*, that lies at first smoa[k]ing in the Heart and Blood, when *Heat* has overcome it (it consisting of such solid particles, which then are put upon motion and agitation) is more strong and vigorous then any thing else that moves in the Blood and Spirits, and comes very near to the nature of the highest *Cordialls* that are." [10]

In most enthusiasts, moreover, the sanguine humor has also grown adust, according to More, who declares "*That a certain Dosis* of Sanguine *mixt with* Melancholy *is the Spirit that usually inspires* Enthusiasts." [11] The enthusiasts, then, are truly "inspired by the spirit," as they were fond of boasting, but the spirit turns out to be nothing higher than the vapors which accompany unnatural melancholy.

The enthusiasts, one might think, are sufficiently degraded by More's discovery that the "inner spirit" consists entirely of melan-

[8] *Enthusiasmus Triumphatus*, p. 7.
[9] *Ibid.*, p. 12.
[10] *Ibid.*, p. 17.
[11] *Ibid.*, p. 15.

cholic vapors; but worse is in store. These vapors, we have seen, could originate in any one of three regions of the body, and on this basis Burton had classified melancholy into three kinds. Only the most humiliating classification for their melancholy, the most contemptible origin for their vapors, would satisfy More in the relentless pursuit of his victims. Their specific disorder he classifies as hypochondriacal or windy melancholy, and as for the origin of their vapors, he declares "that *Enthusiasts* for the most part are intoxicated with vapours from the lowest region of their Body." [12] In his final judgment upon his victims, he writes:

> The *Spirit* then that wings the *Enthusiast* in such a wonderful manner, is nothing else but that *Flatulency* which is in the *Melancholy* complexion, and rises out of the *Hypochondriacal* humour upon some occasional heat, as *Winde* out of an *Aeolipila* applied to the fire. Which fume mounting into the Head, being first actuated and spirited and somewhat refined by the warmth of the Heart, fills the Mind with variety of *Imaginations*, and so quickens and inlarges *Invention*, that it makes the *Enthusiast* to admiration *fluent* and *eloquent*, he being as it were drunk with new wine drawn from that Cellar of his own that lies in the lowest region of his Body.[13]

The weapon against the enthusiasts which More provided in *Enthusiasmus Triumphatus* was soon taken up with a ready will by other Anglican rationalists, particularly More's friends, Glanvill and Rust, and the latter's disciple, Henry Hallywell; and terms long familiar in medical treatises reappeared as stock phrases in the sermons and discourses of these religious apologists. Thus Rust described the raptures of the Puritan fanatics as "so far from the Inspiration of the Holy Spirit, that they are no better then Frenzies and Symptoms of Melancholy, and derive their Original from no higher Principle then the undue Fermentation of the Blood and Spirits." [14] Hallywell echoes More closely in a treatise on the Quakers, where he declares that when

> the Melancholic and Hypochondriacal Humor (which is extraordinarily predominant in them) mixing with the Blood

[12] *Ibid.*, p. 28.
[13] *Ibid.*, p. 12.
[14] *A Discourse of the Use of Reason in Matters of Religion* (London, 1683), p. 33.

and Spirits is somewhat refined in the Heart, and being warmed there, ascends copiously into the Brain, it affects the mind with varieties of Imaginations, and intoxicates and makes the man as it were drunk.[15]

Glanvill, with somewhat more originality, carried More's thesis further by attempting to show that the different moods of the Puritan fanatics depended upon which of their four humors happened at the moment to be adust.[16]

Nowhere else in *A Tale of a Tub* was Swift able to adopt so readily the materials which he came across in reading *Enthusiasmus Triumphatus* as in his use of More's physiological explanation for enthusiasm. For these materials were easily adaptable, in the form in which Swift found them, to his purpose of comic satire. The two principal ingredients of this explanation — More's suggestion that enthusiasm is caused by a "redundancy of vapors" and his discovery of the source of these vapors in the "lowest region" of the body — had been fashioned deliberately as a means of disparagement and ridicule. As such, they were perfectly appropriate for Swift's satire, and he did not hesitate to use them. Swift's madmen and More's enthusiasts share not only the same vapors but the same source of these vapors. Swift's *"Phaenomenon of Vapours*, ascending from the lower Faculties to over-shadow the Brain" is unmistakably hypochondriacal or windy melancholy.

If Swift was content to borrow from More, however, he was not willing to follow his source, as Hallywell had done, with a slavish imitation that amounts to plagiarism. The requirements of a religious satire were not those of a discourse on enthusiasm. In the service of his specific satirical intention, consequently, Swift extends and develops More's analysis of enthusiasm in several directions.

He extends More's analysis in two principal ways. In the first place, he broadens his predecessor's explanation for enthusiasm to take in the activities of conquerors and atheistic philosophers as well. More's discussion of enthusiasm, as we have seen, was confined to two varieties: political and philosophical. He had limited his examples of political enthusiasm to religious fanatics, of philo-

---

[15] *An Account of Familism* (London, 1673), p. 105.
[16] See *A Loyal Tear Dropt on the Vault of Our Late Martyred Sovereign* (London, 1667), pp. 28–29.

sophical enthusiasm to occultists. We noticed in the last chapter that there was a tradition among the Anglican rationalists, shared by More himself, of picturing atheists as a kind of enthusiasts. But this tradition found no place in the specifically anti-Puritan polemics of More, Glanvill, Rust, and Hallywell, which pictured the religious enthusiasts as victims of hypochondriacal melancholy. When the atheists were described as enthusiasts, no attempt was made to account for their disorder by reference to a redundancy of vapors, nor, for that matter, to classify them more particularly as political enthusiasts. When Swift chose to combine these two traditions in which Puritans, on the one hand, and atheists, on the other, were disparaged as enthusiasts, he proceeded to make the atheistic philosophers not only political enthusiasts but victims of hypochondriacal melancholy as well. Furthermore, in portraying both Puritans and atheists as similar to conquerors in their "political ambitions," it was necessary and useful to picture the conquerors themselves as victims of the same disorder.

Secondly, satirical license allows Swift to exaggerate the disorder of his victims and to describe it not as melancholy but as madness. We have noticed a tendency toward hyperbole in the anti-Puritan polemics of the Anglican rationalists themselves, when they describe their antagonists as "mad," or "fit for Bedlam," while the madness of atheism is a frequent theme in their sermons. But we have noticed also that when they come to a clinical discussion of enthusiasm as the effect of a redundancy of vapors they tend to become more accurate and to distinguish the melancholy of enthusiasm from true madness. The term "melancholy" nowhere appears in the "Digression concerning Madness." On the contrary, Swift repeatedly refers to his victims' disorder as "madness," and on several occasions he describes it as a "Distemper" to which we give "the Name of *Madness* or *Phrenzy*." Again, instead of distinguishing enthusiasts from the inhabitants of Bedlam, he emphasizes their essential similarity to these sufferers from madness and frenzy in their literal meaning. Thus, he likens the mad philosophers to "their present undoubted Successors in the *Academy* of *Modern Bedlam*" and suggests that were Epicurus, Descartes, and their like alive "in this our undistinguishing Age" they would "incur manifest Danger of *Phlebotomy*, and *Whips*, and *Chains*, and *dark Chambers*, and *Straw*," a series of restraints and attempted cures to which madmen, not melancholists, were subjected. But what Swift's disparagement of his victims loses in literal accuracy — seldom an important consideration to the satirist — it gains in effectiveness.

Just as Swift extends the boundaries of More's analysis, so he finds it useful for his satirical purpose to develop more fully each of the two principal ingredients of More's analysis: his use of a redundancy of vapors to explain enthusiasm and his suggestion that these vapors originate in the lowest region of the body. More, as we noticed, found these ingredients in Burton's clinical discussion of melancholy in the first part of his famous book. In order to develop these ingredients more fully, Swift seems to have followed the hint offered by More's reference to Burton, if, indeed, he needed any such hint, and to have gone directly to the same source. For one thing, Swift's statement that the mental disorder of conquerors, atheistic philosophers, and founders of new religions is due to "their Dyet, their Education, the Prevalency of some certain Temper, together with the particular Influence of Air and Climate" suggests that he had been reading *The Anatomy of Melancholy* as well as *Enthusiasmus Triumphatus.* "Prevalency of some certain Temper," or combination of humors, we are of course already familiar with as the immediate cause of melancholy. But Swift's allusion to the other, more remote causes of melancholy points to Burton, who had discussed each of them as contributing influences on the malady.[17] More important, the ways in which Swift develops the ingredients of More's analysis of enthusiasm indicate that he probably consulted Burton for further details on the subject of hypochondriacal melancholy.

One of the ways in which Swift develops More's analysis is in the use he makes of the latter's suggestion that the vapors from which enthusiasts suffer have their source in the lower region of the body. This he does in his discussion of Henri IV and Louis XIV as examples of mad conquerors. The purpose served by his introduction of conquerors among the categories of madmen displayed in Section IX is, as we have seen, to enforce his characterization of the other two kinds of madmen as political enthusiasts who share the compulsive ambition of "subduing multitudes" to their own "reasons or visions." But this purpose would have been served quite adequately had Swift merely mentioned conquerors

[17] See *The Anatomy of Melancholy,* I, 2, 2, 1 (diet); I, 2, 4, 2 (education); I, 2, 2, 5 (influence of air and climate).

as a third category of madmen and suggested, as he does, the close similarity between their ambitions and those of introducers of new schemes in philosophy and founders of new religions. The discussion of Henri IV and Louis XIV as typical conquerors, however, serves the quite different purpose of enabling Swift to emphasize and develop, more fully than More had done, the degrading possibilities in the suggestion that it is the lower region of the body that accounts for the redundancy of vapors from which enthusiasts suffer. For the vapors in the brain of Henri IV originated in the lower region of his body, while those of Louis XIV ended there. Although More had not explored such possibilities, Burton had. The exact explanation which Swift offers for the vapors of Henri IV, attributing them to frustrated sexual passion, appears in *The Anatomy of Melancholy*, where it is discussed quite seriously as one of the most virulent causes of hypochondriacal melancholy.[18] In all probability, Swift found it here, realized its possibilities as a means of comic disparagement, and proceeded to apply it to Henri IV.

A second way in which Swift develops More's analysis is in the use he makes of the latter's account of enthusiasm as the product of a redundancy of vapors. More's purpose in accounting for "the Spirit that usually inspires Enthusiasts" by reference to adust humors which had assumed the form of vapors was simply to emphasize his thesis that the "inspiration" boasted of by the fanatics was not supernatural in character and could be explained as a purely natural phenomenon. When he declared more specifically that the spirit "that wings the Enthusiast in such a wonderful manner, is nothing else but that Flatulency which is in the Melancholy complexion, and rises out of the Hypochondriacal humour upon some occasional heat, as Winde out of an Aeolipila applied to the fire," he was simply attempting to offer as degrading an explanation as possible for this "inspiration." By classifying enthusiasm as hypochondriacal or windy melancholy, he was able to suggest that the "Cellar of his own that lies in the lowest region of his Body" was the source of that inspiration which the enthusiast claimed to be supernatural. At the same time More was hinting at further possibilities for disparagement in this classification of which he was clearly aware but did not choose to exploit. The alternative adjectives "hypochondriacal or windy" used to describe

18 See *ibid.*, I, 2, 2, 4.

this species of melancholy were intended to indicate the symptoms as well as the source of this particular disorder. It was from the hypochondrium, or lowest region of the body, that the adust humors originated in this form of melancholy. But since the vapors in this case had so far to travel before they reached the brain, symptoms of flatulency were observable in its victims. More was chiefly interested in the source of these vapors, as well as in their effect upon the enthusiast once they reached his brain, producing in their victim a false assurance of supernatural inspiration. The symptoms which accompanied their transit from hypochondrium to brain he preferred to ignore. Nevertheless, there were obvious possibilities for satire in these symptoms, which Burton had described in some detail in *The Anatomy of Melancholy*.

Swift exploited these possibilities fully in his description of the religious practices of the Aeolists in Section VIII of *A Tale of a Tub*. We noticed in the last chapter one of Swift's reasons for creating this sect. In presenting their beliefs as a reductive system which makes of air or wind a single principle of explanation for the universe, he is able to identify the Puritans with the occultists, since air or wind is a middle term appropriate to both the occultist *anima mundi* and the Puritan "inner spirit." We have noticed also that Swift almost certainly found such an appropriate middle term in the doctrine of Anaximenes as described in Thomas Stanley's *History of Philosophy*. But once we realize that More had attributed the vapors of the enthusiasts to "hypochondriacal flatulency," we are in a position to see why Swift names the members of his sect "Aeolists" and substitutes the term "wind" for that of "air" in Stanley's account of Anaximenes. The peculiar appropriateness of Anaximenes' doctrine and Swift's reason for making it the central belief of his sect are due to the fact that wind is not only a useful middle term applicable to the Aeolists' beliefs but the cardinal symptom of their behavior as well. The members of this sect are Aeolists in practice as well as in belief, for as victims of melancholy they suffer, quite literally, from hypochondriacal flatulency. By following his description of their beliefs with an account of their religious practices, Swift turns from identifying the Puritans with the occultists to picturing their well-known physical contortions in the pulpit and at prayer as the writhings of sufferers from those very "Symptoms of Windy Hypochondriacal Melancholy" to which Burton had devoted an entire chapter of *The Anatomy of Melancholy*.[19] In applying these symptoms to his Aeolists and suggesting that they are deliberate attempts to put into practice the Puritan belief in the central importance of inspiration, Swift turns Burton's serious clinical discussion into the means of comic disparagement.

Swift's attention to founders of new religions in discussing fanaticism and to "introducers of new schemes in philosophy" in discussing atheism, his likening both to military conquerors, and his description of all three forms of madness as "actions that have been performed in the world, under the influence of single men" all imply a clear distinction between leaders and followers where enthusiasm is concerned. His decision to emphasize the role which enthusiasts play as proselytizers had made it inevitable that the causal explanation for enthusiasm which I have been discussing should apply only to the proselytizers themselves, not to their unhappy followers. This emphasis was in keeping with the tradition of Anglican rationalist polemics against fanaticism and atheism which we have been exploring all along. More had limited his attention in *Enthusiasmus Triumphatus* to those fanatics who had established new sects, not to the members of those sects. Glanvill's statement that "he that can be the author of a new kind of madness, shall lead a party" is typical of the repeated stress which the Anglican rationalists placed upon "the contriving, as well as the propagating of new religions," in Swift's phrase, as the phenomenon which they described as the effect of melancholy. The followers of these false preachers they were content to describe as "poor deluded people," more to be pitied than reprehended, the cause of whose conversion was dismissed as mere gullibility. Similarly, in attacking atheism the Anglican rationalists distinguish between "speculative atheists" and "practical atheists."[20] The former, formulators of atheistic systems like Epicurus or Hobbes, are those who are branded as madmen and enthusiasts. The latter, who find it convenient to espouse the beliefs popularized by speculative atheists, are accounted for by a much simpler explanation. Practical atheists profess a disbelief in God, not because of mental aberration, but because of moral depravity. "For when men once indulge themselves in wicked courses," Tillotson explained to his

[19] See *ibid.*, I, 3, 2, 2.
[20] For a typical use of this distinction, see Tillotson's sermon on "The Wisdom of Being Religious," *Works* (London, 1820), I, 317–89.

congregation, "the vicious inclinations of their minds sway their understandings, and make them apt to disbelieve those truths which contradict their lusts."[21] Similarly, Swift, speaking of the practical atheist in his *Letter to a Young Gentleman Lately Entered into Holy Orders*, declares "that the Trade of *Infidelity* hath been taken up only for an Expedient to keep in Countenance that universal Corruption of *Morals*, which many other Causes first contributed to introduce, and to cultivate" (IX, 80). The followers of atheistic philosophers, then, as well as the victims of false preachers, were exempt from the physiological cause attributed by Swift and his predecessors to the zeal of their leaders.

Yet Swift required for his satirical purpose a causal explanation for the success of these proselytizers which would be as "physical" or "mechanical" and, hence, as absurd and contemptible as the causal explanation for their zeal which he found in his "phenomenon of vapors." Since neither Burton nor More could offer him any help here, he produced explanations of his own devising.

The first of these explanations seeks to account for the manner whereby the fanatic preachers, who as sufferers from hypochondriacal flatulency derived their "inspiration" from within, were able to communicate this "inspiration" to their congregations, who, since they did not share the same disorder with their preachers, were forced to reproduce the same symptoms by artificial means. A part of the description of the religious practices of the Aeolists in Section VIII is devoted to this explanation. Here Swift describes various mechanical contrivances and other artificial means for disploding the "spirit," consistently equated with wind, among the faithful and for introducing it quite literally into the gaping members of the Puritan congregations.

This "mechanical" explanation assumes of course that the followers of the fanatic preachers have already been converted. It is because they have become devoted proselytes of these leaders that they seek to share their "inspiration." What still remains to be suggested is an explanation, as purely "natural" as all the others, for the indisputable fact that enthusiastic leaders so readily attract a following. And, in Section IX of *A Tale of a Tub*, Swift provides the reader with a natural or mechanical cause for the success of enthusiasts in winning proselytes. At the conclusion of his discus-

[21] *Ibid.*, I, 393.

sion of "the great Introducers of new Schemes in Philosophy," he writes:

> · Let us therefore now conjecture how it comes to pass, that none of these great Prescribers, do ever fail providing themselves and their Notions, with a Number of implicite Disciples. And, I think, the Reason is easie to be assigned: For, there is a peculiar *String* in the Harmony of Human Understanding, which in several individuals is exactly of the same Tuning. This, if you can dexterously screw up to its right Key, and then strike gently upon it; Whenever you have the Good Fortune to light among those of the same Pitch, they will by a secret necessary Sympathy, strike exactly at the same time. And in this one Circumstance, lies all the Skill or Luck of the Matter; for if you chance to jar the String among those who are either above or below your own Height, instead of subscribing to your Doctrine, they will tie you fast, call you Mad, and feed you with Bread and Water [I, 105–6].

This explanation for the success of Epicurus, Descartes, and their like in finding willing disciples appears at first sight to be a brilliant but purposely obscure play of wit on Swift's part. Brilliant it certainly is, for it carries the disparaging suggestion that the disciples of these philosophers have assented to their doctrines, not because of the rhetorical powers of their authors nor because of the inherent credibility of these theories, but because of the physical condition of the disciples themselves. But it could have been obscure to few of Swift's contemporaries, for whom an explanation based upon a theory of "secret necessary Sympathy" carried a wealth of degrading associations with "sympathetic magic," Sir Kenelm Digby's notorious "sympathetic powder," and numerous other quack nostrums and theories which had been exploded by this time. Swift's musical metaphor which portrays the similarity of temperament between enthusiastic philosophers and their disciples as a "hidden harmony" between musical instruments is openly reminiscent of the view of the universe as a vast musical instrument which had been popular among astrologers and occultists earlier in the seventeenth century. As one of these writers had suggested:

> If we look more narrowly into the great fabrick or machine, we shall find that it is a *Pamphoniacal* and musical instru-

ment, and every individual creature is as a several cord or string indued with a distinct and various tone, all concurring to make up a catholick melody, and every one of these understanding the sound and tune of each other, otherwise the *Harmony* would be discordant, and man himself makes up one string of this great instrument.[22]

What is particularly interesting about this extravagant theory which Swift offers the reader is not simply the degrading associations it carries but the fact that it is used as a natural or mechanical explanation for a phenomenon which, he implies, might otherwise remain inexplicable: the fact that the authors of such mad theories should succeed in imposing them upon others. For within the terms of the explanation he suggests, it follows that the acceptance by one person of another man's theories, whether mad or sane, is an inevitable consequence of the "secret necessary Sympathy" existing between these two individuals. Now it happens that Swift had come across just such an explanation for just such a phenomenon a short while before in the course of his reading. We have noticed that during his residence at Kilroot in 1695 and 1696 Swift had read with considerable irritation Glanvill's youthful effusion, *Scepsis Scientifica*, which "old Mr. Dobbs" had loaned him. At one point in this book, Glanvill undertakes "to shew how rashly we use to conclude things *impossible*," by instancing "some reputed *Impossibilities*, which are only strange and difficult performances." The first of these seeming impossibilities was "the power of one man's imagination upon anothers," which, although difficult to understand, was attested sufficiently by various stories.

That the *Phancy* of one Man should *bind* the Thoughts of another, and determine them to their particular objects, will be thought *impossible*: which yet, if we look deeply into the matter, wants not it's probability. . . . I see not why the *phancy* of one man may not determine the cogitation of another rightly qualified, as easily as his *bodily motion*. Nor doth this influence seem more unreasonable, then that of one *string* of a Lute upon another, when a *stroak* on it causeth a proportionable motion in the *sympathizing* consort, which is distant from it and not sensibly touched.[23]

[22] John Webster, *Academiarum Examen* (London, 1654), pp. 28–29.
[23] *Scepsis Scientifica* (London, 1665), pp. 146–47.

That "this kind of secret influence may be advanc't to so strange an operation in the Imagination of one upon another, as to fix and determine it" can be explained quite readily, Glanvill goes on to suggest, if one accepts "the *possibility* of mechanically solving the *Phaenomenon*." The "*Mechanical* account" which he proceeds to offer reads in part as follows:

> . . . the agitated pars [sic] of the Brain begetting a *motion* in the proxime *Aether*; it is propagated through the liquid *medium*; as we see the motion is which is caus'd by a stone thrown into the water. And when the thus moved *matter* meets with any thing like that, from which it received its primary *impress*; it will in like manner move it; as it is in *Musical strings* tuned *Unisons*. And thus the motion being convey'd, from the *Brain* of one man to the *Phancy* of another; it is there receiv'd from the instrument of conveyance, the *subtil* matter; and the same kind of *strings* being moved, and much what after the same manner as in the first *Imaginant*; the *Soul* is awaken'd to the same apprehensions, as were they that caus'd them.[24]

If Swift found this irritating, he must have been amused as well at Glanvill's perfectly serious suggestion that his "Mechanical account" would clear up any difficulty in understanding "the power of one man's imagination upon another's." In suggesting that Swift adopted Glanvill's explanation, I do not wish to imply that he was attempting to parody a passage in *Scepsis Scientifica* which few of his readers would have recognized. He was simply turning to his own purposes of comic satire a "mechanical account" which, in attempting to explain how "the Phancy of one Man should bind the Thoughts of another," provided him with a remarkably appropriate causal explanation for the success of enthusiasts in winning proselytes.

The peculiar appropriateness of Glanvill's theory for Swift's satirical purpose is due to more than the mere fact that here was a "mechanical account" which could be used to disparage atheistic philosophers by suggesting that their success in winning disciples was due to natural causes rather than to their rhetorical powers or the inherent probability of their doctrines. What was at least

[24] *Ibid.*, p. 148.

equally appropriate for Swift's purpose was the fact that Glanvill's theory was offered as an explanation for a specific phenomenon described as "the power of one man's imagination upon another's." For Swift proceeds to explain a little later in Section IX that it is precisely because of the power of one man's imagination upon another's that enthusiasts of every kind have succeeded in finding proselytes, since enthusiasm itself, he explains, is an effect of the imagination. In providing such an explanation, he turns from the discussion of the physiological causes of enthusiasm and of its successful promotion to take up the psychological causes of these same phenomena.

Swift's discussion of the psychological causes of the appearance and spread of enthusiasm is comparatively brief. It is limited to two substantial paragraphs which directly follow and, indeed, depend upon the much longer discussion of the physiological causes of enthusiasm which I have just discussed. In the context of the full title of Section IX, "A Digression concerning the Original, the Use and Improvement of Madness in a Commonwealth," it is clear that these two closely related series of causes — physiological and psychological — constitute the "original" of madness, while the extended proposal "to furnish Employment for this Redundancy of *Vapour*," which concludes the section and does not pertain to religion, constitutes the "use and improvement of madness in a commonwealth."

In spite of its comparative brevity, however, no single portion of *A Tale of a Tub* provokes so much interest for, or offers such rewards to, the historian of ideas as Swift's discussion of the psychological causes of enthusiasm. Its importance, therefore, calls for greater attention to this crucial portion of the book than its length would seem to warrant. Because the two paragraphs in which Swift presents this discussion deal with different aspects of the same subject and appear at first sight to contradict each other, it will be necessary to take them up separately, though in the order in which they appear in *A Tale of a Tub*.

In the first of these two paragraphs, Swift declares that if one accepts the definition of madness as "a Disturbance or Transposition of the Brain, by Force of certain *Vapours* issuing up from the lower Faculties; Then has this *Madness* been the Parent of all those mighty Revolutions, that have happened in *Empire*, in *Philosophy*, and in *Religion*." He proceeds:

For, the Brain, in its natural Position and State of Serenity, disposeth its Owner to pass his Life in the common Forms, without any Thought of subduing Multitudes to his own *Power*, his *Reasons* or his *Visions*; and the more he shapes his Understanding by the Pattern of Human Learning, the less he is inclined to form Parties after his particular Notions; because that instructs him in his private Infirmities, as well as in the stubborn Ignorance of the People. But when a Man's Fancy gets *astride* on his Reason, when Imagination is at Cuffs with the Senses, and common Understanding, as well as common Sense, is Kickt out of Doors; the first Proselyte he makes, is Himself, and when that is once compass'd, the Difficulty is not so great in bringing over others; A strong Delusion always operating from *without*, as vigorously as from *within* [I, 108].

It will be noticed that the psychological cause of enthusiasm is introduced as a final "proof" of the theory, already expounded, that "vapors issuing up from the lower faculties" are the physiological cause of this phenomenon. This "proof" consists in inferring the assumed cause from the observed effect. Enthusiasm is defined as self-delusion accompanied by a strong desire of "bringing over others" to the same delusion. Delusion is assent to a chimera of the imagination. In order for such chimeras to be accepted as true by the enthusiast, his brain must have undergone some serious disturbance which has permitted his imagination or fancy to usurp the place of reason. So serious a disturbance of the brain implies the presence of some such physiological cause as the force of vapors. But a disturbance of the brain produced by vapors is called madness. Therefore, enthusiasm is madness.

We are already familiar with the conclusion of this sorites. Its premises are what call for examination here, particularly the view of the enthusiast as a victim of the imagination and the belief that the force of the imagination is the necessary middle link in the chain of causes that leads back to vapors as the ultimate explanation for enthusiasm. It need hardly be a matter for surprise that here, as so often elsewhere, Swift's premises are to be found in *Enthusiasmus Triumphatus*. More writes:

The Originall of such peremptory delusions as mankind are obnoxious to, is the enormous strength and vigour of the *Imagination*; which Faculty though it be in some sort in our power, as *Respiration* is, yet it will also work without our leave . . . and hence men become mad and fanaticall whether they will or no.[25]

That enthusiasm was primarily a delusion, the result of accepting the chimeras of the imagination as true, seemed to More self-evident; his suggestion that this was due to melancholic vapors was simply an assumed physiological cause, as plausible as it was degrading, for the obvious psychological disturbance from which enthusiasts suffered.

> Now what it is in us that thus captivates our *Imagination* [he explained], and carries it wide away out of the reach or hearing of that more free and superiour Faculty of *Reason*, is hard particularly to define. But that there are sundry *material* things that do most certainly change our Mind or Phansy, experience doth sufficiently witnesse.[26]

Hence he proceeded to suggest as the most important of these material causes the pathological condition of melancholy with its accompanying vapors.

More's view that in enthusiasm the imagination is carried "wide away out of the reach or hearing of that more free and superior faculty of reason," or, as Swift puts it, "a man's fancy gets astride on his reason," assumes a mutual opposition between the faculties of reason and imagination whereby the dominance of one entails the subjection of the other. Swift's description of enthusiasm as a psychological condition in which "imagination is at cuffs with the senses, and common understanding, as well as common sense, is kicked out of doors" carries the antithesis further. Where the fancy, or imagination, has usurped the place of reason, the senses and common understanding cease to play their appropriate roles. This dichotomy in which common understanding and the senses serve under the banner of reason and help oppose fancy is explained by an important passage in *Enthusiasmus Triumphatus*.

> By *Reason* I understand so settled and cautious a Composure of Mind as will suspect every high-flown & forward Fancy that endeavours to carry away the assent before deliberate examination; she not enduring to be gulled by the vigour

[25] *Enthusiasmus Triumphatus*, p. 5.
[26] *Ibid.*

123

or garishnesse of the representation, nor at all to be born down by the weight or strength of it; but patiently to trie it by the known Faculties of the Soul, which are either the *Common notions* that all men in their wits agree upon, or the *Evidence of outward Sense*, or else a *clear and distinct Deduction from these*. Whatever is not agreeable to these three, is *Fancy*, which testifies nothing of the *Truth* or *Existence* of any thing, and therefore ought not, nor cannot be assented to by any but mad men or fools.[27]

The external senses, then, as well as common notions, or common understanding, are standards against which reason judges the truth of the phantasms of the imagination and rejects those which are false. Every man's imagination presents these false phantasms or chimeras to his mind. But as long as the brain is "in its natural position and state of serenity," with reason in control, there is no danger that these products of the fancy will be accepted as true against the clear evidence of common notions and the external senses. If, on the other hand, More explains, a chimera

> were *so strong* as to bear it self against all the occursions and impulses of *outward* Objects, so as not to be broken, but to keep it self entire and in *equall* splendour and vigour with what is represented from *without*, and this *not arbitrariously*, but *necessarily* and *unavoidably* . . . the Party thus affected would not fail to take his own Imagination for a reall Object of Sense.[28]

This is what has happened to the enthusiast, whose mind has "become obnoxious to such disturbances of *Melancholy*, in which she has quite lost her own Judgement and freedome, and can neither keep out nor distinguish betwixt her own Fancies and reall Truths." [29] Thus the enthusiast while awake is in the same condition as the normal man asleep, who believes his dreams to be real. Melancholy in the one case, as sleep in the other, has rendered impotent the ordinary standards by which chimeras can be seen to be false. For it is only when "the *evidence* of the *outward senses* be shut out by *sleep* or *melancholly*," Glanvill wrote later,

[27] *Ibid.*, pp. 38–39.
[28] *Ibid.*, p. 4.
[29] *Ibid.*, p. 2.

echoing More, that "we *believe* those *representations* to be *real* and *external transactions*, when they are only *within* our *heads*; Thus it is in *Enthusiasms*, and *Dreams*." [30]

Once we perceive this tradition of portraying enthusiasm as a waking dream or delusion in which the enthusiast accepts the chimeras of his fancy as true because his "imagination is at cuffs with the senses," we can understand why Swift describes both the Aeolists, or Puritans, and the "atheistic" cosmologists, such as Epicurus and Descartes, as exponents of reductive systems. Both groups, as he describes them, betray a tendency to believe strongly in a chimera which is contradicted by all the evidence of the senses and of common understanding and to reduce all "real and external transactions," attested by the senses and the understanding, under this simple chimera afforded by the imagination. Such a tendency corresponds to that described by Swift in Section I of *A Tale of a Tub*, "The Introduction," where, in referring to the "*pretended Virtue of Numbers*" believed in by the occultists, he writes of

> that prudent Method observed by many other Philosophers and great Clerks, whose chief Art in Division has been, to grow fond of some proper mystical Number, which their Imaginations have rendred Sacred, to a Degree, that they force common Reason to find room for it in every part of Nature; reducing, including, and adjusting every *Genus* and *Species* within that Compass, by coupling some against their Wills, and banishing others at any Rate" [I, 34–35].

For the fondly cherished beliefs of founders of new religions and of introducers of new schemes in philosophy are "fancies" or chimeras of the imagination quite as unreal as the "proper mystical number" within whose compass the occultists reduce, include, and adjust "every genus and species." Neither the Divine mission boasted by the religious fanatic nor the atheistic cosmology invented by Epicurus or Descartes has any connection with "real and external transactions." In the case of the religious fanatic, this is all too obvious. If the imagination, More writes, can prove so strong in some individuals as to assure them

> of the presence of some externall Object which yet is not there, why may it not be as effectual in the begetting of the belief of

[30] *A Blow at Modern Sadducism* (4th ed., London, 1668), pp. 101–2.

some more internall apprehensions, such as have been reported
of mad and fanaticall men, who have so firmly and immutably
fancied themselves to be *God the Father*, the *Messias*, the *Holy
Ghost*, the *Angel Gabriel*, the *last and chiefest Prophet* that
God would send into the world, and the like? [31]

Such notions as these, commonly attributed to many of the
founders of new sects which had made their appearance during the
sixteenth and seventeenth centuries, were chimeras in the strictest
sense, since they had no basis in reality.

Swift pictures the systems of the atheistic cosmologists as
chimeras of the very same kind in *A Tale of a Tub*. He introduces
his discussion of these men in general, and of Epicurus and
Descartes in particular, in Section IX with these words:

> LET us next examine the great Introducers of new Schemes
> in Philosophy, and search till we can find, from what Faculty
> of the Soul [imagination] the Disposition arises in mortal
> Man, of taking it into his Head, to advance new Systems with
> such an eager Zeal, in things agreed on all hands impossible
> to be known: from what Seeds this Disposition springs [va-
> pors], and to what Quality of human Nature [secret necessary
> sympathy] these Grand Innovators have been indebted for
> their Number of Disciples [I, 104–5].

Taken out of its proper context, this condemnation of philosophers
for advancing "new systems with such an eager zeal, in things
agreed on all hands impossible to be known" can be interpreted
as that fideist attitude toward the speculations of all philosophers
which Dryden expressed in *Religio Laici*:

> In this wilde Maze their vain Endeavours end.
> How can the *less* the *Greater* comprehend?
> Or *finite Reason* reach *Infinity*?
> For what cou'd *Fathom God* were *more* than *He* [ll. 38–41].

Yet, within its proper context, the meaning of Swift's statement
is clearly so different from Dryden's as to carry an implicit contradiction of the poet's view. It is not for having followed the guidance of "finite reason" but for having abandoned it in favor of
the imagination that Swift condemns these philosophers. The sys-

[31] *Enthusiasmus Triumphatus*, p. 4.

tems of Epicurus and Descartes advance "things agreed on all hands impossible to be known," not because the origin of the universe cannot be known — a view which as an expression of philosophical agnosticism contradicts Swift's views on natural religion which we examined in chapter ii — but because the particular atheistic or "semi-atheistic" theories regarding the universe which Swift attributes to Epicurus and Descartes are fantastic "fancies," or chimeras of their own imaginations, and consequently "impossible to be known." Swift is simply employing a paradox here which was not uncommon in the Anglican rationalist polemics against atheism. Tillotson, for example, assured his congregation that "the atheist is unreasonable, because he pretends to know that which no man can know, and to be certain of that which nobody can be certain of; that is, that there is no God." [32] It is impossible to know that there is no God, since every reasonable man knows that God exists. Similarly, such theories as those advanced by Epicurus and Descartes, which sought to explain the origin of the universe without reference to God or to Divine Providence, were equally impossible to be known, since all reasonable men acknowledged the Divine origin and government of the universe as an indisputable fact. Such wild theories, therefore, could only be explained as chimeras, products of a disordered imagination in which their authors had come to believe as the result of delusion.

We are in a position now to understand the meaning of the term "new" which Swift repeats so frequently in Section IX ("new schemes in philosophy," "new systems," "new religions") in describing the chimerical fancies to which enthusiasts have succumbed and have sought to make others succumb. The term "new" here does not mean "modern," nor does it carry any temporal connotation at all. It carries, instead, the connotation of "novelty" or "singularity." At the same time, this term is contrasted, not with "old" in any temporal sense, much less to "ancient," but to what Swift describes as the "common forms." At the beginning of the paragraph which we are examining, Swift sets up a contrast between two modes of behavior which is meant to parallel the contrast between reason and imagination already noticed. The brain "in its natural Position and State of Serenity," that is, when reason

[32] *Works*, I, 360.

127

is in proper control of the faculties, "disposeth its Owner to pass his Life in the common Forms, without any Thought of subduing Multitudes to his own *Power*, his *Reasons* or his *Visions*." Again, "the more he shapes his Understanding by the Pattern of Human Learning, the less he is inclined to form Parties after his particular Notions." This is because the pattern of human learning "instructs him in his private Infirmities, as well as in the stubborn Ignorance of the People." We are offered a dichotomy, then, in which new schemes in philosophy, new systems, and new religions appear under the banner of imagination and are described as "particular notions" and "private infirmities" in order to stress their novelty and singularity. In opposition to these, and under the banner of reason, appear "common forms," "pattern of human learning," and, ironically, "stubborn ignorance of the people." These common forms are simply the "consensus gentium," or universal agreement of mankind, to which the Anglican rationalists were fond of appealing and in which a common agreement on basic religious beliefs could be found wherever reason had remained undisturbed by imagination. It is "the same Belief in Things Invisible" to which, Swift declares in Section IX, "all Mankind would unhappily be reduced" were it not for the "blessings" of enthusiasm.

The common forms which the religious fanatics have ignored in founding new sects are simply the beliefs and manner of worship accepted by the members of the national church. To reject what most men accept in this respect and to try to introduce new beliefs or new forms of worship is always dangerous, for it probably stems from error and it inevitably leads to civil strife. To acquiesce in the religion professed by the rest of the nation, on the other hand, will certainly promote peace and will almost as certainly guard one from the dangerous delusions of the imagination. This was why Swift could not share the Puritan sympathy for the Huguenots and other Protestant minorities in Catholic countries. In promoting the cause of Protestantism in a country where the common form of religion was Catholicism, these dissenters were simply deluding themselves and others into believing that religious reform and not civil disturbance was their real goal. In *The Sentiments of a Church-of-England Man* (1708), Swift writes:

> WHEN a *Schism* is once spread in a Nation, there grows, at length, a Dispute which are the Schismaticks. Without en-

tering on the Arguments, used by both Sides among us, to fix the Guilt on each other; it is certain, that in the Sense of the Law, the *Schism* lies on that Side which opposeth it self to the Religion of the State. I leave it among *Divines* to dilate upon the Danger of *Schism*, as a Spiritual Evil; but I would consider it only as a Temporal one. And I think it clear, that any great Separation from the established Worship, although to a new one that is more pure and perfect, may be an Occasion of endangering the publick Peace; because, it will compose a Body always in Reserve, prepared to follow any discontented Heads, upon the plausible Pretexts of advancing *true Religion*, and opposing Error, Superstition, or Idolatry. For this Reason, *Plato* lays it down as a Maxim, that *Men ought to worship the Gods, according to the Laws of the Country*; and he introduceth *Socrates*, in his last Discourse, utterly disowning the Crime laid to his Charge, of *teaching new Divinities*, or Methods of Worship [II, 11–12].

He goes on to condemn the Huguenots in France, the Puritans in England, and the Arminians in Holland for having opposed the established worship in their respective countries.

There is nothing in this view which is inconsistent with Swift's belief in the importance of reason in religion, which was discussed in chapter ii. As I pointed out in that place, the Anglican rationalists, when they emphasized the necessity for human reason in interpreting Scripture, carefully distinguished between two separate senses in which the individual ought to be guided by reason. Only in reference to those basic beliefs of the Christian religion which are absolutely necessary to salvation was the individual's private judgment a sufficient guide. On all other points of belief and worship, it was the reason of his teachers which ought to serve as the individual's guide in religion. Similarly, in his sermon "On the Testimony of Conscience," Swift assures his congregation that

God hath placed Conscience in us to be our Director only in those Actions which Scripture and Reason plainly tell us to be good or evil. But in Cases too difficult or doubtful for us to comprehend or determine, there Conscience is not concerned; because it cannot advise in what it doth not understand, nor decide where it is itself in doubt: But, by God's great Mercy, those difficult Points are never of absolute Necessity to our Salvation [IX, 150–51].

Now the Anglican rationalists were willing to concede that even in Catholic countries all the "fundamentals of Christian religion" were believed, even though the divines of these countries had "built hay and stubble upon the foundation of Christianity." Therefore, no appeal to private judgment could justify the creation of new sects and the leading of others into dissent, for as Tillotson remarked:

> I cannot think (till I be better informed, which I am always ready to be) that any pretence of conscience warrants any man, that is not extraordinarily commissioned, as the apostles and first publishers of the gospel were, and cannot justify that commission by miracles as they did, to affront the established religion of a nation (though it be false) and openly to draw men off from the profession of it, in contempt of the magistrate and the law.[33]

The "common forms" or "pattern of human learning" which the atheistic cosmologists have ignored in devising their chimerical theories concerning the origin of the universe, on the other hand, denote, not the established form of worship of any particular country, but simply the universal acknowledgement of God's existence, the Divine origin of the universe, and the other components of natural religion which have been common among philosophers of every nation and era, except for those few whose desire for singularity and novelty has led them to devise new schemes and new systems in the face of the "consensus gentium." Since it is reason which has led the majority of philosophers to accept the truths of natural religion, as is testified by their common consent on this subject, the "Grand Innovators," as Swift calls the atheistic philosophers, must have had recourse to their imaginations to provide themselves with such monstrous notions as violate all the testimony of reason. Swift's characterization of these men as seekers after novelty and singularity who have succumbed to the credulity of the imagination is a favorite theme of Anglican rationalist polemics against atheism. Such beliefs as the existence

[33] *Ibid.*, II, 458 59.

of God, Divine Providence, and the immortality of the soul, Tillotson preaches,

> are so far from being singular opinions, that they are and always have been the general opinion of mankind, even of the most barbarous nations. Insomuch, that the histories of ancient times do hardly furnish us with the names of above five or six persons who denied a God. And Lucretius acknowledgeth that Epicurus was the first who did oppose those great foundations of religion, the providence of God, and the immortality of the soul.

But the atheistic philosopher in his desire for singularity "pretends to be wiser than to believe any thing for company; he cannot entertain things upon those slight grounds which move other men." And so he invents novel theories which are as ridiculous as they are unreasonable. He imagines, for example,

> either that the heavens and the earth, and all things in them, had no original cause of their being, or else that they were made by chance, and happened he knows not how to be as they are; and that in this last shuffling of matter, all things have by great good fortune fallen out as happily and as regularly as if the greatest wisdom had contrived them, but yet he is resolved to believe that there was no wisdom in the contrivance of them.

Reason was never responsible for such novelties as these.

> And it is a wonder [Tillotson remarks], that there should be found any person pretending to reason or wit that can assent to such a heap of absurdities, which are so gross and palpable that they may be felt. So that if every man had his due, it will [sic] certainly fall to the atheist's share to be the most credulous person, that is, to believe things upon the slightest reasons.[34]

No great change was necessary on Swift's part to transform these authors of a "heap of absurdities" to which they assented against the testimony of all reasonable men into the mad "Grand Innovators" of Section IX of *A Tale of a Tub* who have ignored the "pattern of human learning" in order to follow "particular notions"

[34] *Ibid.*, I, 374–76.

which are but the chimeras of their own fancy. It was simply a matter of combining two polemical traditions and of applying More's explanation for the delusion of religious fanatics to the atheistic philosophers as well, so that the atheistic cosmologist, quite as much as the religious fanatic, emerges as a man whose fancy has gotten "astride on his reason" as the result of a "disturbance or transposition of the brain, by force of certain vapours."

More's psychological explanation for enthusiasm, however, was limited like his physiological explanation for the same phenomenon to the founders of sects and leaders of parties. Just as Swift added to More's physiological explanation for the disorder of these proselytizers by finding causes of a similar character for their success in winning converts, so here he proceeds to invent a psychological explanation of his own to account for the widespread acceptance of these chimerical theories which their authors owed to their own disordered imaginations. He does so by explaining that, if the proselytizers themselves have succumbed to the delusive power of the imagination through necessity, their willing disciples have done the same thing by choice. Having explained that the "thought of subduing multitudes to his own power, his reasons or his visions" is for the enthusiast himself an inevitable consequence of the pathological disturbance of the brain which accompanies melancholy and leads to the ascendance of his imagination, so that "the first Proselyte he makes, is Himself," Swift then goes on to declare that "when that is once compass'd, the Difficulty is not so great in bringing over others; A strong Delusion always operating from *without*, as vigorously as from *within*." His explanation for the ease with which the enthusiast brings over others to a delusion which is accepted as willingly by them as by himself is as follows:

> For, Cant and Vision are to the Ear and the Eye, the same that Tickling is to the Touch. Those Entertainments and Pleasures we most value in Life, are such as *Dupe* and play the Wag with the Senses. For, if we take an Examination of what is generally understood by *Happiness*, as it has Respect, either to the Understanding or the Senses, we shall find all its Properties and Adjuncts will herd under this short Definition: That, *it is a perpetual Possession of being well Deceived.* And first, with Relation to the Mind or Understanding; 'tis mani-

fest, what mightly Advantages Fiction has over Truth; and the Reason is just at our Elbow; because Imagination can build nobler Scenes, and produce more wonderful Revolutions than Fortune or Nature will be at Expence to furnish. . . . Again, if we take this Definition of Happiness, and examine it with Reference to the Senses, it will be acknowledged wonderfully adapt. How fade and insipid do all Objects accost us that are not convey'd in the Vehicle of *Delusion*? How shrunk is every Thing, as it appears in the Glass of Nature? So, that if it were not for the Assistance of Artificial *Mediums,* false Lights, refracted Angles, Varnish, and Tinsel; there would be a mightly Level in the Felicity and Enjoyments of Mortal Men [I, 108–9].

Since those who join enthusiastic sects and accept enthusiastic schemes in philosophy do not share the madness of their leaders, they still have the use of reason but choose to ignore it. They prefer the deceptions of the imagination to the discoveries of reason because delusion itself is a euphoric existence which they actively seek and eagerly experience. Among those who would rather enjoy the happiness provided by pleasant dreams than suffer the rude shock of awakening to reality, the enthusiast, Swift suggests, will always find willing disciples, for his stock consists entirely of such delusions. Therefore, the difficulty is never "so great in bringing over others," once he has made a proselyte of himself, for his eager followers gladly will ignore the evidence of those very standards of the understanding (common notions) and the senses (sensible phantasms) which stand ready to prove the chimeras of the imagination false. So great, on the contrary, are the advantages of the imagination where delusion is desired that the chimerical fancies which that faculty can furnish are accepted by the followers of enthusiasm not merely in spite of, but because of, the fact that they are contradicted by the unwelcome evidence of the understanding and the senses.

In the second and concluding paragraph which he devotes to the psychological causes of enthusiasm, Swift proceeds to examine a second advantage which the imagination enjoys over reason in affording delusion to those who seek happiness in "a perpetual possession of being well deceived." He writes:

In the Proportion that Credulity is a more peaceful Possession of the Mind, than Curiosity, so far preferable is that Wisdom, which converses about the Surface, to that pretended Philosophy which enters into the Depth of Things, and then comes gravely back with Informations and Discoveries, that in the inside they are good for nothing. The two Senses, to which all Objects first address themselves, are the Sight and the Touch; These never examine farther than the Colour, the Shape, the Size, and whatever other Qualities dwell, or are drawn by Art upon the Outward of Bodies; and then comes Reason officiously, with Tools for cutting, and opening, and mangling, and piercing, offering to demonstrate, that they are not of the same consistence quite thro'. Now, I take all this to be the last Degree of perverting Nature; one of whose Eternal Laws it is, to put her best Furniture forward. . . . from all which, I justly formed this Conclusion to my self; That whatever Philosopher or Projector can find out an Art to sodder and patch up the Flaws and Imperfections of Nature, will deserve much better of Mankind, and teach us a more useful Science, than that so much in present Esteem, of widening and exposing them (like him who held *Anatomy* to be the ultimate End of *Physick*.) And he, whose Fortunes and Dispositions have placed him in a convenient Station to enjoy the Fruits of this noble Art; He that can with *Epicurus* content his Ideas with the *Films* and *Images* that fly off upon his Senses from the *Superficies* of Things; Such a Man truly wise, creams off Nature, leaving the Sower and the Dregs, for Philosophy and Reason to lap up. This is the sublime and refined Point of Felicity, called, *the Possession of being well deceived*; The Serene Peaceful State of being a Fool among Knaves [I, 109–10].

In this paragraph as in the preceding one, Swift suggests that there are two modes of behavior available to men in their search for that to which they give assent. One consists in "that wisdom, which converses about the surface," while the other consists in "that pretended Philosophy which enters into the depth of things." Here is a dichotomy as rigid as that of the preceding paragraph, but it appears at first sight to be of an altogether different kind. Indeed, the two paragraphs seem to contradict each other. In the first paragraph, an opposition was suggested between imagination or fancy on the one hand, and reason on the other. Under the banner of reason were listed not only common understanding but the senses as well, with which the imagination was described as being "at cuffs" in taking over the role of reason. In the second paragraph, on the other hand, it is the senses themselves which are opposed to reason. In both paragraphs reason is ironically condemned as the enemy of delusion, but the source of delusion itself is presented first as the imagination and then as the senses.

This is only an apparent contradiction. Swift has not shifted the target of his satire. He is still satirizing enthusiasm as a delusion of the imagination. In this paragraph quite as much as in the preceding one, he continues to explore the "advantages" which the imagination enjoys in preference to reason for those who seek to be deceived. The only difference is that in the first paragraph he examines one kind of delusion which the imagination can provide, and in the second paragraph he points out a different kind of self-deception afforded by hearkening to the imagination instead of to reason.

We must remember that in spite of radically different attitudes on the importance and reliability of the imagination, there was common agreement in the seventeenth century about the nature of the imagination. It is a faculty or internal sense which is the source of the phantasms which the mind receives. Now these phantasms are of two kinds. The first kind are produced or invented by the imagination itself. The second are received into the imagination from the external senses and are in turn presented by the imagination to the mind. The first are merely chimeras or fancies and have no counterpart outside the imagination which is their ultimate source. The second are the sensible qualities of external objects and testify to the existence of these objects which have been perceived by the senses. It is the first kind of phantasm, "such as dupe and play the wag with the senses," which Swift discusses in his first paragraph. The second kind, sensible phantasms which the imagination owes to the external senses, are the subject of his second paragraph.

Each of these two classes of phantasm offers a quite different kind of delusion to the person who hearkens to the imagination instead of to reason. The first kind — chimeras — are guilty of material falsity. They claim real existence for that which has no existence outside the imagination itself. Here the question, then, is simply whether there exists any counterpart to these phantasms. Any normal man in a waking state can determine this question easily by reference to the standards provided by the understanding and the external senses. If the chimera takes the form of some "internal apprehension," such as that the individual has been commissioned by God to found a new religion or that the universe came into existence without the help of any Divine agency, it can be judged false by reference to the common notions in the understanding; for these notions, being true, will contradict the fancy by failing to provide any counterpart for it. If, on the other hand, the chimera takes the form of a pretended sensible phantasm, such as that of a centaur, it can be judged false by the senses, which will testify that no such material object exists outside the imagination.

The second kind of phantasm provided by the imagination — the sensible qualities of actually existing external objects derived from the senses — offers an altogether different type of delusion to the person who ignores reason in his pursuit of the imagination. These phantasms are guilty of formal falsity. They testify correctly to the existence of external objects, but they give a false picture of their real nature. Here the external senses can offer no help in correcting the false picture, for they are the source of these deceptive, though actual, sensible phantasms. Only reason can be of aid, by piercing beneath these sensible qualities, or accidents, which dwell "upon the outward of bodies," and discovering the real nature, or substance, of these bodies.

But the man who, like the followers of enthusiastic sects and systems, chooses to ignore his reason and to attend only to his imagination is in no position to do this. Noting only the sensible phantasms which his imagination has received from his senses, he identifies sensible qualities with the bodies to which they adhere, and the result is delusion as complete as, though of a different kind from, that which follows from assenting to chimeras. Favoring credulity in place of curiosity, seeking delusion rather than truth, such a man, Swift writes, prefers "that wisdom, which converses about the surface, to that pretended philosophy which enters into the depth of things." He chooses to rely entirely upon the information of his senses, such as sight and touch, which "never examine farther than the color, the shape, the size, and whatever other qualities dwell, or are drawn by art upon the outward of bodies," and to equate these outward qualities, or accidental appearances, with the inward natures of bodies. He can ignore the contrary testimony of reason, which offers "to demonstrate, that they are not of the same consistence quite through," and "can with Epicurus content his ideas with the films and images that fly off upon his senses from the superficies of things." When the imagination can offer such advantages for delusion as these, in addition to the chimeras of its own invention, it is small wonder that he who equates felicity with "the possession of being well deceived" should prefer this faculty to reason or that he should follow so eagerly after the enthusiastic leader whose fancy has gotten astride his reason. There is a remarkable congruity between these two, the enthusiast and his disciple, for if the former is a madman, the latter is a fool. He has arrived at the "serene peaceful state of being a fool among knaves."

If this conclusion is Swift's own, the premises from which he reaches it are not. They are the common ingredients of Anglican rationalist polemics against atheism — more specifically, of their frequent attacks on materialism and on Epicurean sensationalism which served as its support.

The sensationalism of Epicurus to which Swift alludes was described by Cudworth as follows: "The *Democritick* and *Epicurean Atheists*, Universally agree in this, that not only *Sensations*, but also all the *Cogitations* of the *Mind*, are the meer *Passions* of the *Thinker*, and the *Actions* of *Bodies* Existing without, upon him." It was the teaching of Epicurus and Democritus, Cudworth explains,

> that *Sense* is Caused by certain Grosser *Corporeal Effluvia*, streaming from the Surfaces of Bodies Continually, and entering through the *Nerves;* But that all other *Cogitations of the Mind*, and mens either sleeping or waking *Imaginations*, proceed from another sort of *Simulachra, Idols* and *Images*, of a more Fine and Subtle Contexture, coming into the Brain, not through those open Tubes, or Channels of the Nerves, but immediately through all the smaller Pores of the Body: so that, as we never have *sense* of Any thing, but by means of those *Grosser Corporeal Images*, obtruding themselves upon the *Nerves*; so have we not the least *Cogitation* at any Time in our *Mind* neither, which was not *Caused* by those *Finer Cor-*

137

poreal Images, and *Exuvious Membranes,* or *Effluvia,* rushing upon the *Brain,* or *Contexture of the Soul.*" [35]

All thought, then, is sensation, although some of these corporeal images are of a grosser, some of a finer, nature.

This theory reveals two features which any churchman would find objectionable as lending support to atheism and against which the Anglican rationalists in particular directed a great part of their apologetics. For as we noticed earlier of their opposition to his cosmology, the concern of the Anglican rationalists with Epicurean sensationalism reflected far more than an antiquarian interest in the errors of ancient paganism. It was Hobbes who had revived the sensationalism of Epicurus and had given it fresh currency in the later seventeenth century, and it was at Hobbes that these divines were striking in their polemics against Epicurus.

The first objectionable feature in this theory was the notion that we have "not the least cogitation at any time in our mind which was not caused by those finer corporeal images rushing upon the brain." For these corporeal images originate in "bodies existing without," and, if the entire stock of our ideas consists in such images as these, we can have no idea of anything but bodies. In other words, we can have no idea of God. Cudworth, attacking this notion "That we can have no *Idea, Conception,* or *Thought* of any thing, not *Subject to Sense;* nor the least *Evidence* of the *Existence* of any thing, but from the same," continues:

> Thus a Modern *Atheistick Writer; Whatsoever we can conceive, hath been Perceived first by Sense, either at once or in parts; and a man can have no Thought representing any thing not Subject to Sense.* From whence it follows, that whatsoever is not *Sensible* and *Imaginable,* is utterly *unconceivable* and to us *Nothing.*[36]

The "modern atheistic writer" is of course Hobbes, and the italicized statement a direct quotation from the *Leviathan,* in which Hobbes is arguing that "there is no Idea, or conception of any thing we call *Infinite.*" [37] Such a notion undermined the entire

[35] *The True Intellectual System of the Universe* (London, 1678), p. 850.

[36] *Ibid.,* p. 634.

[37] *Leviathan, or the Matter, Forme, & Power of a Common-Wealth Ecclesiasticall and Civill* (London, 1651), p. 11.

foundation for natural religion and raised in its place the specter of philosophical agnosticism. In order to counter so dangerous a theory, the Anglican rationalists answered by asserting that many of our ideas, including that of God, are not sensations at all, nor are they derived in any way from sense.

It is a sign there is little of Reason left [Stillingfleet writes], where Sense is made the only Umpire of all kinds of Beings. Must all intellectual Beings be proscrib'd out of the order of Nature, because they cannot pass the scrutiny of Sense? . . . If God were to be try'd by the judgment of Sense, he must cease to be God; for how can an infinite and spiritual Being be discern'd by the judgment of Sense? and if he be not an infinite and spiritual Being, he is not God.[38]

Therefore the idea of God must be of an altogether different character from sensations and have an entirely different origin from sense. For "corporeal Phantasms," Stillingfleet explains,

are so far from helping us in forming this Idea, that they alone hinder us from a distinct Conception of it, while we attend to them; because these bear no proportion at all to such a Being. So that this Idea however must be a pure act of Intellection, and therefore supposing there were no other faculty in Man but Imagination, it wo ud [sic] bear the greatest repugnancy to our Conceptions, and it wou'd be according to the Principles of *Epicurus* and some modern Philosophers, a thing wholly impossible to form an Idea of GOD, unless with *Epicurus* we imagin him to be Corporeal, which is to say, he is no God. . . . it thereby appears that there is a higher faculty in Man's Soul than mere imagination.[39]

This faculty of reason is not only distinct from imagination, but it owes nothing to it for its conceptions.

The other objectionable feature in Epicurean sensationalism which lent support to atheism was the notion that "we never have sense of anything, but by means of those grosser corporeal images, obtruding themselves upon the nerves." For if the notion that our most refined conceptions can only pertain to bodies led to agnosticism, the notion that our ideas of bodies themselves are only "cor-

[38] *Origines Sacrae* (7th ed.; Cambridge, 1702), p. 255.
[39] *Ibid.*, pp. 250–51.

poreal effluvia, streaming from the surfaces of bodies" led to materialism. Man's soul itself must be material if he must "content his ideas with the films and images that fly off upon his senses from the superficies of things." In order to counter this theory, the Anglican rationalists answered by stressing the deceptiveness of the senses and of the sensible phantasms which they convey to the imagination, while at the same time they asserted that there is an immaterial principle in man — his reason — which in virtue of its superiority to matter can correct the false appearances which the imagination has received from the senses. "Now what is the principle that controls our senses, and corrects the deception of them?" Tillotson asks.

> If the soul of man be mere matter, it can only judge of things according to the impressions which are made upon our senses: but we do judge otherwise, and see reason to do so many times. Therefore it must be some higher principle, which judges of things not by the material impressions which they make upon our senses, but by other measures. And therefore, to avoid this inconvenience, Epicurus was glad, to fly the absurdity, to affirm, that all things really are what they appear to us, and that in truth the sun is no bigger than it seems to be." [40]

If, then, with Epicurus, we judge of external bodies according to "the films and images that fly off upon the senses from the superficies of things," we invite deception by hearkening only to appearances. Reason, the immaterial principle in man, is essential, not only for our ideas of immaterial beings, but for our ideas of the right natures of material beings as well.

> Nothing can render the *Philosophy* of *Epicurus* more justly suspected to any rational and inquisitive Mind [Stillingfleet writes], than his making the Senses the only conveyors of the truth of things to the Mind. . . . For if my Mind affirms every thing to be in its proper nature according to that Idea which the Imagination hath receiv'd from the impressions upon the organs of Sense, it will be impossible for me ever to understand the right natures of things. . . . So that in reference even to the grossest material Beings, it must be the

[40] *Works*, VII, 570.

Perception only of the Mind, which can truly inform us of their proper Nature and Essence.[41]

And Cudworth writes that

> had not these Atheists been Notorious Dunces . . . they would clearly have learn'd from thence, That *Sense* is not *Knowledge* and *Understanding*, nor the *Criterion* of Truth as to *Sensible* things themselves; it reaching not to the *Essence* or *Absolute Nature* of them, but only taking notice of their *Outside*, and perceiving its own *Passions* from them, rather than the Things themselves: and That there is a Higher Faculty in the Soul, of *Reason* and *Understanding*, which judges of Sense, detects the *Phantastry* and *Imposture* of it; discovers to us that there is nothing in the Objects themselves like to those forementioned *Sensible Ideas*; and resolves all Sensible Things into *Intelligible Principles*.[42]

These are, of course, the very premises of Swift's paragraph contrasting "that wisdom, which converses about the surface" with "that pretended philosophy which enters into the depth of things." His description of the senses which "never examine farther than the color, the shape, the size, and whatever other qualities dwell, or are drawn by art upon the outward of bodies" fits precisely Cudworth's condemnation of the senses for "reaching not to the essence or absolute nature" of things, "but only taking notice of their outside." And his description of reason as a faculty which offers to demonstrate that these bodies "are not of the same consistence quite through" corresponds exactly to Cudworth's view of reason as a higher faculty which "discovers to us that there is nothing in the objects themselves" corresponding to the sensible qualities reported by the senses.

Once we perceive the source of these premises of Swift's in the tradition of Anglican rationalist polemics and notice the close connection between materialism and "that wisdom, which converses about the surface," or sensationalism, we are in a position to understand the peculiar appropriateness of "clothing" as the single principle upon which the tailor-worshippers, in Section II of *A Tale of a Tub*, found their entire system. The tailor-worship-

[41] *Origines Sacrae*, pp. 267–68.
[42] *True Intellectual System*, p. 635.

pers can find no place in their system for anything else but that which covers the "outward of bodies" because as materialists they are believers in Epicurean sensationalism and content their ideas with "the films and images that fly off upon their senses from the superficies of things." Theirs is a reductive system of a somewhat different kind from that of the religious fanatics and atheistic cosmologists which we noticed a little earlier. They reduce "every genus and species," not to a chimerical fancy which has no existence outside the imagination, but to the grossly deceptive sensible phantasms with which their imagination provides them. Thus they reduce the whole to one of its infinitesimal parts — a part which has real existence but is of a very limited character. These "philosophers" have succumbed to the same kind of delusion as did another such philosopher described by Swift in his *Remarks upon a Book, Intitled, "The Rights of the Christian Church"*:

> I REMEMBER some Years ago a Virtuoso writ a small Tract about Worms, proved them to be in more Places than was generally observed, and made some Discoveries by Glasses. This having met with some Reception, presently the poor Man's Head was full of nothing but Worms; all we eat and drink, all the whole Consistence of human Bodies, and those of every other Animal, the very Air we breathe; in short, all Nature throughout was nothing but Worms: And by that System, he solved all Difficulties, and from thence all Cases in Philosophy [II, 76].

Just as this unfortunate man identified every part of the universe with worms, so the tailor-worshippers, or materialists, seek to reduce all existence to the sensible qualities which dwell upon the "outward of bodies."

In Section II, of course, where the tailor-worshippers appear, Swift's target is materialism itself. It would be a mistake, however, to conclude that because the premises which appear in Swift's discussion of the imagination in Section IX were derived from Anglican rationalist polemics against materialism he is therefore satirizing materialism there also in contrasting "that wisdom, which converses about the surface" with "that pretended philosophy which enters into the depth of things." On the contrary, he is satirizing enthusiasm of every kind as a delusion of the imagination, and if those atheistic enthusiasts who are materialists choose to enjoy that particular delusion which comes from attending exclusively to the sensible phantasms of the imagination, this faculty has other advantages, equally fruitful of delusion, to offer those who, like the religious fanatics and the atheistic cosmologists, seek theirs in the fancies or chimeras of the imagination. Whereas the Anglican rationalists make use of these premises concerning the deceptiveness of the senses and of the sensible phantasms of the imagination in order to undermine the sensationalism of Epicurus and Hobbes and to assert the spirituality of the soul, Swift uses them for an altogether different purpose: to suggest that since no faculty enjoys so many advantages for delusion as the imagination, and no man is so helplessly indebted to the imagination for his systems and sects as the enthusiastic leader, therefore he will always find willing disciples among those who seek happiness in a "perpetual possession of being well deceived."

For Swift, then, the premises which he found in the Anglican rationalist polemics against atheism were simply commonplaces which he accepted as such and repeated in a quite different context from that in which he had found them. What is most remarkable about these premises is the uncompromising epistemological dualism which governs every one of his assumptions and determines the nature of his judgments. Two modes of thinking, two ways of assent, directly opposed to each other in every respect, are available, Swift assumes, to mankind. The first is that of reason, which leads to truth, and is characteristic of those who shape their thinking by the "pattern of human learning," or *consensus gentium*. The other is that of the imagination, which leads only to delusion, and is characteristic of those who succumb to enthusiasm, whether as leaders or as disciples. The same epistemological dualism shapes the apologetics of the Anglican rationalists, "there being two main wayes whereby our mind is wonne off to assent to things," as More explained in an appendix to *Enthusiasmus Triumphatus*, "viz. The *guidance of Reason*, or *The Strength and vigour of Fancy*." [43] Or, as his friend George Rust expressed the notion, "the Spirit as 'tis a Principle of Knowledge in us, is

[43] "Mastix His Letter to a Private Friend," *Enthusiasmus Triumphatus* (London, 1656), p. 294. This epistle is omitted from the later, more readily available edition of *Enthusiasmus Triumphatus* from which I have been quoting.

either Internal Sense [imagination] or Reason." [44] If this were truly a commonplace, as Swift seems to have assumed that it was, there would be no justification for believing that Swift's reading of Anglican rationalist apologetics was a necessary condition for its appearance in *A Tale of a Tub*. But it is not a commonplace, even among all of those Anglican divines who, from Hooker's time down to Swift's own day, espoused the importance of reason in religion. It is, on the contrary, a weapon of apologetics which was peculiar to those divines whom I have been calling the "Anglican rationalists." In adopting epistemological dualism as a weapon with which to combat atheism, they set themselves a course which took them far from Hooker, to whom, as we noticed in chapter ii, they were indebted in so many other respects.

For Hooker, a dualism which opposes reason to imagination as two antagonistic faculties is not only meaningless but impossible. It is a basic assumption of Hooker's that "men, if we view them in their spring, are at the first without understanding or knowledge at all. . . . The soul of man being therefore at the first as a book, wherein nothing is and yet all things may be imprinted" (I, vi, 1). He accepts without question the Thomistic theory of knowledge and all it implies. If the soul of man is at first an *abrasa tabula*, or blank slate, this is because there is, according to the Scholastic formula, "*nihil in intellectu quod non prius in sensu.*" Reason, then, is wholly dependent upon the senses for all of its ideas, and since nothing can come to it from the senses but by way of the imagination, reason is equally dependent upon the imagination. This is not to say, of course, with the sensationalists that "a man can have no thought representing anything not subject to sense," for "by reason," Hooker writes, "man attaineth unto the knowledge of things that are and are not sensible" (I, vii, 1). It is to say, however, that all of the "higher cogitations" of which reason is possessed, including the idea of God and all the principles of natural religion, have come to it by the same avenues of sense and imagination as have served for its perception of material objects. "Those properties of God and those duties of men towards him" which are the ingredients of natural religion are "conceived by attentive consideration of heaven and earth" (III, viii, 6). In other words, the idea of God is arrived at by a posteriori demonstration from natural effects to their supernatural cause, while the

[44] *Discourse of the Use of Reason*, p. 35.

144

axioms of Natural Law have no place in our minds until others have proposed them and we have assented to them instinctively. Axioms such as "God to be worshipped" and "parents to be honoured," Hooker writes, "as soon as they are alleged, all men acknowledge to be good; they require no proof or further discourse to be assured of their goodness. Notwithstanding whatsoever such principle there is, it was at the first found out by discourse, and drawn from out of the very bowels of heaven and earth" (I, viii, 5). Imagination, then, is not a delusive faculty, nor the senses a source of deception; on the contrary, they are essential to every operation of the mind. "The mind," Hooker writes, "while we are in this present life, whether it contemplate, meditate, deliberate, or howsoever exercise itself, worketh nothing without continual recourse unto imagination, the only storehouse of wit and peculiar chair of memory" (V, lxv, 7).

There were not a few Anglican divines of the Restoration era who advanced the claims of natural religion upon such an empirical basis as Hooker had assumed. Whereas Hooker, who was not concerned with disproving atheism in the *Laws*, had taken such matters for granted, that group known to history as the "physico-theologians," including such prominent figures as John Wilkins, Samuel Parker, and John Ray, met the challenge of atheism by developing an elaborate series of teleological arguments for the existence of God and for the Divine origin of the universe. Like Hooker, they assumed that "nothing is in the intellect which was not first in the senses," and they concentrated exclusively, therefore, upon the argument from design and drew all of their proofs from our experience and the evidence of our senses.

The Anglican rationalists, however, suspected that Hooker's assumption that the soul of man is "at the first as a book, wherein nothing is and yet all things may be imprinted" stood too close to the sensationalism revived by Hobbes to offer any help in combating the materialism which the author of the *Leviathan* derived from his theory of knowledge. They could perceive no essential difference, indeed, between the two and could condemn, therefore, in the same sentence the doctrine of the sensationalists "that they have not the least *Cogitation* of any thing, not subject to *Corporeal Sense*" and the Scholastic formula accepted by Hooker "that there is nothing in *Humane Understanding* or *Conception*, which was not First in *Bodily Sense*; a Doctrine," Cudworth remarked, "highly favourable to *Atheism*."[45] Just as they rejected Hooker's distinction between reason and faith to meet the needs of an apologetics against Catholicism which Hooker had not foreseen, so the need for an apologetics which would serve them in combating a revived materialism led the Anglican rationalists to reject Hooker's empirical theory of knowledge. They were "rationalists," indeed, in the philosophical sense; for as supporters of a theory that reason is a separate source of knowledge, superior to and independent of the senses and the imagination, they were altogether distinct from those contemporary empiricists — the physico-theologians — who also emphasized the importance of reason in religion, but on quite different grounds.[46]

What the Anglican rationalists required was a theory of knowledge fashioned in such a way as to make those two principles of religion which the sensationalism of Hobbes denied — the spirituality of the human soul and the idea of God in the soul — the two most certain truths to which we are capable of giving assent. Just such a theory of knowledge had been provided by Descartes. He too had been unable to perceive any essential difference between sensationalism and the empiricism of the schools. In the *Discourse on Method* (1637), he had written:

> The reason why many are persuaded that there is difficulty in knowing [that there is an idea of God in our minds which is at least as certain as any demonstration of geometry can possibly be], as also in knowing what their soul is [a substance not dependent on any material thing and entirely distinct from the body], is that they never raise their minds above the things of sense, and that they are so accustomed to consider

[45] *True Intellectual System*, p. 636.

[46] As a means of classifying all seventeenth-century epistemologies, the popular dichotomy of empiricism versus rationalism is inexact and misleading, for it tends to group into a single category such diverse figures as the physico-theologians and the followers of Hobbes. As a means of distinguishing between two groups of Anglican divines, both of whom emphasized the importance of natural religion, however, it is both accurate and useful. It should be clear that by empiricism I mean something quite different from sensationalism. For a severe criticism by a physico-theologian of the grounds upon which the Anglican rationalists supported natural religion, see Samuel Parker, *A Demonstration of the Divine Authority of the Law of Nature, and of the Christian Religion* (London, 1681), pp. 5–7.

nothing except what they can image (a mode of thinking restricted to material things), that whatever is not imageable seems to them not intelligible [the doctrine of the sensationalists]. Even the philosophers in their schools do so, as is sufficiently manifest from their holding as a maxim [the Scholastic formula] that there is nothing in the understanding which was not previously in the senses, where, however, it is certain, the ideas of God and of the soul have never been. . . . In any case, neither our imagination nor our senses can ever assure us of anything whatsoever save so far as our understanding intervenes.[47]

Thus, if these two principles of religion do not receive the recognition they deserve, the fault is attributable to erroneous theories of knowledge which, whether sensationalist or empiricist, fail to offer them any support. Nothing is more certain than these two principles, however, once we accept the dualistic theory of knowledge which he proposes, according to which many of our ideas have never been in the senses at all, having originated in the understanding itself, while neither our imagination nor our senses can assure us of anything at all, even of that which pertains to corporeal things, except by the intervention of the understanding.

In 1641, ten years before the *Leviathan* appeared, Descartes expanded these notions, only sketched in the fourth part of his *Discourse*, into a full-length treatise, the *Meditationes de Prima Philosophia*, in which, as the title went on to assert, *Dei Existentia et Animae Humanae a Corpore Distinctio Demonstratur*.[48] Here was a metaphysics which, as if by providential design, offered to demonstrate the same two religious questions which Hobbes was to challenge a decade later and to do so in such a certain manner that "no longer will anyone dare to doubt either the existence of God or the real and veritable distinction in man between soul and body." [49]

It is hardly surprising that the Anglican rationalists should have felt that the *Meditations* offered them just the weapon they needed for meeting the challenge of Hobbes's materialism, nor that they

[47] *Descartes' Philosophical Writings*, trans. Norman Kemp Smith (London, 1952), p. 144.
[48] That is to say, in all editions beginning with the second (1642).
[49] *Descartes' Philosophical Writings*, p. 187.

should have taken over, practically intact, the Cartesian demonstrations for the existence of God and the spirituality of the soul as well as the epistemological dualism which served as support for these demonstrations. For More the decade during which he employed the arguments and assumptions of the *Meditations* in his own writings as a means of refuting Hobbes was the 1650's. In this period immediately following the appearance of the *Leviathan*, he wrote *An Antidote against Atheism* (1652), which Marjorie Nicolson has called "More's first Cartesian treatise," and *The Immortality of the Soul* (1659), in each of which he addressed his attention to one of the two most objectionable features of Hobbes's sensationalism.[50] Between these two "Cartesian treatises" he wrote *Enthusiasmus Triumphatus*, which, although it is not devoted to atheism, reflects to a strong degree Descartes' epistemological dualism. Again, Cudworth's great treatise against atheism, his *True Intellectual System*, makes use of the arguments and assumptions of the *Meditations* to such an extent that his most recent commentator, J. A. Passmore, declares that it is "not misleading to call Cudworth a Cartesian, so great was their agreement on many vital issues." On no issue were the two in more complete agreement than in their common dualism. "Indeed," Mr. Passmore remarks, "Cartesian influence penetrates every nook and cranny of Cudworth's epistemology."[51] Finally, substantial portions of Stillingfleet's *Origines Sacrae*, from which I have been quoting, are simply paraphrases of Descartes' arguments and conclusions in the *Meditations*. In short, if the Anglican rationalists were unanimous in condemning Descartes' physics for offering support to atheism, as we noticed in the last chapter, they were no less unanimous in finding his metaphysics and his epistemology remarkably useful for attacking the same target.

None of the arguments which the Anglican rationalists took over from Descartes' *Meditations* stand closer to their original than that by which they attempt to prove that sensation is not

[50] See Marjorie Nicolson, "The Early Stage of Cartesianism in England," *Studies in Philology*, XXVI (1929), 356–74. This article includes an excellent study of More's debt to Descartes and of his later reaction against him. For his friend Glanvill's indebtedness to Descartes, see Jackson I. Cope, *Joseph Glanvill, Anglican Apologist* (St. Louis, Mo., 1956), *passim*.

[51] *Ralph Cudworth: An Interpretation* (Cambridge, 1951), pp. 8, 11 ff.

knowledge and that "in reference even to the grossest material beings, it must be the perception only of the mind which can truly inform us of their proper nature and essence," the basic premise also, we noticed, of Swift's contrast between "that wisdom, which converses about the surface" and "that pretended philosophy which enters into the depth of things." It is in the second of his *Meditations* that Descartes presents this argument. He is trying to prove that the soul or, which is the same for Descartes, the mind is entirely distinct from the body, because thought is the essential attribute of mind, while nothing that pertains to thought is an attribute of body. In order to prove this, he must show "that, properly speaking, bodies are cognised not by the senses or by the imagination, but by the understanding alone," since sense and imagination pertain to the body. The example he chooses by which to illustrate this point is the celebrated piece of wax. He describes the wax as it is when

it has been but recently taken from the hive; it has not yet lost the sweetness of the honey it contained; it still retains something of the odour of the flowers from which it has been gathered; its colour, its shape, its size, are manifest to us; it is hard, cold, easily handled, and when struck upon with the finger emits a sound. [But] let it be moved towards the fire. What remains of the taste exhales, the odour evaporates, the colour changes, the shape is destroyed, its size increases, it becomes liquid, it becomes hot and can no longer be handled, and when struck upon emits no sound. Does the wax, notwithstanding these changes, still remain the same wax? We must admit that it does; no one doubts that it does, no one judges otherwise. What, then, was it I comprehended so distinctly in knowing the piece of wax? Certainly, it could be nothing of all that I was aware of by way of the senses, since all the things that came by way of taste, smell, sight, touch and hearing, are changed, and the wax none the less remains. [Nor could it be anything that I was aware of by way of the imagination. For the mental images I can form of the wax pertain also only to its color, its shape, its size, and the like.] Consequently this comprehension of it cannot be the product of the faculty of imagination. . . . I must, therefore, admit that I cannot by way of images comprehend what this wax

is, and that it is by the mind alone that I apprehend it. . . .
And what has especially to be noted is that our apprehension
of it is not a seeing, nor a touching, nor an imaging, and has
never been such, although it may formerly have seemed so,
but is solely an inspection of the mind. [Apprehension in this
sense, that is to say, thought, is attributable to the human
mind alone. For when I perceived the wax by the external
senses and even by the imaginative faculty,] what did I apprehend that any animal might not have seen? When, however,
I distinguish the wax from its external forms; when stripped
as it were of its vestments I consider it in complete nakedness,
it is certain that though there may still be error in my judgment, I could not be thus apprehending it without a mind
that is human.[52]

This is essentially the same argument that we noticed in the
statements by Cudworth and Stillingfleet, for example, which I
quoted earlier as parallels to Swift's paragraph contrasting "that
wisdom, which converses about the surface" with "that pretended
philosophy which enters into the depth of things." But, then, to the
same degree and extent that Descartes' argument parallels that of
Cudworth and Stillingfleet, it also parallels the premises of Swift's
somewhat different argument. Why, then, ought we to assume
that Swift took his premises from the Anglican rationalist polemics against atheism rather than from the *Meditations* itself? It is
true that there is no evidence for Swift's ever having read Descartes, but this in itself proves nothing. Nevertheless, there is a
very good reason for believing that Swift was indebted for his
premises here to the Anglican rationalists rather than to Descartes.
For if there are elements which all three share in common, there
are other elements shared by Swift and the Anglican rationalists
which we do not find in Descartes. I refer to the disparaging reference which Swift makes to Epicurus and to his ironical praise of
those people — obviously sensationalists — who follow "that wisdom which converses about the surface" and "can with Epicurus
content [their] ideas with the films and images that fly off upon
[their] senses from the superficies of things." For Descartes' *Meditations* is philosophical discourse, not religious apologetics. He
propounds his own "philosophy which enters into the depth of

[52] *Descartes' Philosophical Writings*, pp. 208–10.

things" but says nothing of "that wisdom, which converses about the surface"; since it was no part of his purpose to attack a sensationalism which still had to await its revival for another ten years. It is the Anglican rationalists, and they alone, who, in taking over Descartes' arguments as part of their polemics against Hobbes, balance the one theory of knowledge against the other and find as much to say in disparagement of Epicurus and his sensationalist teachings as in favor of the idealism of Descartes.

Swift's epistemological premises in *A Tale of a Tub*, then, are Cartesian, but they are Cartesian only at second hand. Indeed, there is no reason to believe that the young man who had declared to his cousin a short while before that "to enter upon causes of philosophy is what I protest I will rather die in a ditch than go about" was so much as aware that his premises were Cartesian or that Descartes figured in the Anglican rationalist apologetics which he had been reading in any other way than as the formulator of a cosmology which was roundly denounced for lending support to atheism. And, if Swift was ignorant of the history of these ideas to the extent that he was unaware of their origin, he seems to have been equally unaware of their fate. For the fact is that Swift's premises in Section IX were not only far less common than he apparently realized but they had already become somewhat outdated by the time he started to write *A Tale of a Tub*.

At the conclusion of chapter ii, I pointed out that Anglican rationalism rapidly declined into obscurity in the 1690's because of a change in the climate of controversy which called for a new apologetics at the same time that it rendered the apologetics developed by the Anglican rationalists inappropriate and unnecessary. I drew attention to the fact that the rapid eclipse of Catholicism as a threat to the Establishment following the revolution of 1688 was one important cause which contributed toward making the apologetics of the Anglican rationalists obsolete. In the same fashion, and at almost the same time, their elaborate apologetics against materialism, in the form in which it had been revived by Hobbes, became needless. With the appearance of Locke's *Essay concerning Human Understanding* in 1690 and the widespread acceptance of the empiricism expounded in that book, the crude sensationalism which Hobbes had taught ceased to play any important part in religious controversy. At the same time, the enormous popularity of Locke's empiricism was accompanied by a simultaneous decline in the popularity of the Cartesian theory of knowledge, and as a result an apologetics based upon the epistemology of Descartes was no longer acceptable or convincing to many Englishmen.[53] For it is a curious fact that in spite of important differences between Locke and Hooker the demise of Anglican rationalism a hundred years after Hooker had laid its foundations was accompanied by Locke's reassertion of the only two important tenets of Hooker's which the later Anglican rationalists had rejected: the basic distinction between knowledge and faith and the empirical basis of all human knowledge.[54] Stillingfleet, the only one of the Anglican rationalists discussed in this book who was still alive when Swift wrote the religious satire of *A Tale of a Tub*, took exception to both these tenets in his famous controversy with Locke.[55] But he himself illustrates, in a remarkable fashion, the radical shift in apologetics which had taken place by the time Swift started to write *A Tale of a Tub*. In 1697, the year after Swift finished his religious satire and thirty-five years after he himself had written *Origines Sacrae*, Stillingfleet began a new book with the same title and the same general purpose of combating atheism as his earlier book. A new *Origines Sacrae* was called for, not only because the kind of atheists to whom Stillingfleet's earlier book was addressed — Hobbes and the other sensationalists — no longer posed any serious threat, but because the Cartesian arguments which played so important a part in the first *Origines Sacrae* were no longer effective. Stillingfleet did not live to complete his new book, but, in the hundred pages or so which he wrote, he severely criticized Descartes' proofs for the

[53] See Sterling P. Lamprecht, "The Role of Descartes in Seventeenth-Century England," *Studies in the History of Ideas,* III (New York, 1935), 181–240.

[54] Locke's assertion of the empirical basis of all human knowledge is too well known to require comment. His assertion of the basic distinction between knowledge and faith is less well known and appears in his second letter to Stillingfleet. He writes: "Faith stands by itself, and upon grounds of its own; nor can be removed from them, and placed on those of knowledge. Their grounds are so far from being the same, or having any thing common, that when it is brought to certainty, faith is destroyed; it is knowledge then, and faith no longer" (*The Works of John Locke* [London, 1823], IV, 146).

[55] For a study of this and other controversies in which Locke was involved as a result of his *Essay,* see John W. Yolton, *John Locke and the Way of Ideas* (London, 1956).

existence of God from the idea of God in the human mind — the principal proofs in the first *Origines Sacrae* — and declared that the most convincing proof for the existence of God was the argument from design, which such empiricists as Wilkins, Parker, and the other physico-theologians had been offering for years, but which had played only a minor role in Stillingfleet's earlier book, as in all the Anglican rationalist treatises against atheism.

The religious satire of *A Tale of a Tub*, then, was already somewhat old-fashioned when Swift wrote it. It ridiculed Catholicism and Puritanism at a time when neither was any longer a serious threat to the Establishment, and it used conventions for attacking the former which had been popular before the Revolution and conventions for attacking the latter which had been devised during the Commonwealth period in the midst of a situation of ecclesiastical affairs which was just the opposite of that which obtained in Swift's own day. Again, it attacked atheism under forms which no longer posed any serious threat to religion, for not only had materialism in the form of Hobbes's sensationalism dwindled in importance but the cosmology of Descartes had suffered a fate similar to that of his epistemology in popular estimation. And the attack was based, finally, upon premises which were no longer current at the time Swift was writing. Aristotle, summoned to appear before Gulliver by the sorcerers of Glubbdubdrib, expressed his satisfaction that "the Doctrine of *Epicurus*" and "the *Vortices* of *Descartes*, were equally exploded" (XI, 181). He might have added that this was no recent fate and that Gulliver's creator had been flogging many a dead horse in his first venture into satire.

Chapter 5

THE ORIGIN OF
A TALE OF A TUB

We have seen that a specific tradition of Anglican apologetics — the Anglican rationalist polemics against Catholicism, Puritanism, and atheism — was the immediate religious and philosophical background of Swift's satire on abuses in religion in *A Tale of a Tub* in the same sense, and to as great a degree, as the Temple-Wotton and Phalaris controversies were, by common consent, the immediate background of his satire on abuses in learning in the same book. Just as the proximate occasion for the latter satire was Swift's residence with, and friendship for, Temple during the very period in which the ancients-moderns dispute was most intense, making it inevitable that he should become acquainted with the contributions of both parties to the quarrel, so the proximate occasion for Swift's religious satire was, it is almost impossible to doubt, his decision to take Anglican orders and the necessary course of reading to which this decision lead.

In view of the fairly abrupt change in the climate of Anglican apologetics during the 1690's which I traced at the end of the last chapter, it would be convenient if we could assume that Swift did a good part, at least, of the reading in preparation for his ordination in the 1680's, while he was a student at Trinity College. Although he certainly had not made any definite decision to take orders at this date, the alternatives open to him were so few that he must already have considered the possibility, at least, of such a future step. And if the study of divinity were customary at Trinity among undergraduates and resident bachelors who contemplated taking orders, there would be a distinct possibility that Swift's reading of religious controversy had begun well before the change in Anglican apologetics which took place in the 1690's.

It was apparently not uncommon at about this time for students at Oxford and Cambridge who intended to become candidates for ordination to begin their study of divinity shortly after matriculation. Several pamphlets addressed to such students testify to this fact. Daniel Waterland's *Advice to a Young Student*, written in 1706, and Bishop Thomas Wilson's *Instructions for an Academic Youth*, written in 1727, were both drawn up to fill the need of undergraduates at the two universities who intended to combine some of their reading for ordination with their classical and philosophical studies for the bachelor's degree. Both authors make clear, however, that their undergraduate readers ought to devote most of their attention at this time to their classical and philosophical studies. "I therefore allow all other Time, except *Sundays*, and *Holidays*, to these," Waterland writes, "and *them* to Divinity." [1] Such reading in divinity as they recommend, furthermore, while fairly extensive for the amount of time allotted, is simply preparatory for the more serious study necessary to qualify for ordination. The reading consists mostly of Scripture, a few books of devotion, and numerous sermons — both authors consider four hundred sermons a respectable number for the undergraduate to have read and abridged by the time he commences B.A. With such a beginning, however, it would still be necessary, once the student had received his degree, to apply himself "wholly to *Divinity* for some Time" before proceeding to orders. Such intense application as this was often necessary for undergraduates at the two English universities "because," Waterland explains, "many design for *Orders*, soon after they take a Degree, and must therefore be prepar'd in that Time, or not at all." [2]

The situation at Trinity College, Dublin, was somewhat different from that which obtained at Oxford and Cambridge. Undergraduates at Trinity matriculated earlier than did those at the two English universities. The average age at which students entered Trinity was sixteen or seventeen. The canonical age for ordina-

[1] Daniel Waterland, *Advice to a Young Student. With a Method of Study for the Four First Years* (2nd ed.; London, 1730), p. 12.
[2] *Ibid.*, p. 12.

tion to the diaconate was twenty-three, to the priesthood twenty-four. Consequently, since the average student contemplating ordination was still some seven years from his goal at the time of his matriculation, there was no need for the conscientious sermon-reading to which the English student was expected to devote his Sundays, holidays, and time before retiring at night ("and you will not sleep the worse," Wilson remarks).[3] Instead, students at Trinity were expected to spend the full seven years of residence required for the M.A. in studying the academic subjects required by the statutes. The course of study at Trinity enjoined by the Laudian statutes of 1637 required students to devote their first four years to classical and philosophical subjects exclusively. Greek and Latin authors they read privately with their tutors, while philosophy was the subject of public lectures: on Porphyrius' *Isagoge* the first year, on Aristotle's *Organon* the second year, on his *Physics* the third year, and on his *Metaphysics* and *Ethics* the fourth year. After commencing B.A., resident bachelors pursued these studies further during the last three years, with the addition of Hebrew, mathematics, and Aristotle's *Politics*. Only after qualifying for the M.A., seven years after first matriculating at the university, did candidates for ordination normally begin the private study of divinity.[4]

Swift was considerably younger than the average student when he entered Trinity. He was only fourteen at the time of his matriculation in 1682. Ordination was still ten years away, and he had by no means decided definitely upon such a goal. He re-

[3] Thomas Wilson, "Instructions for an Academic Youth," *Works* (Oxford, 1863), VII, 180. Not all English students were old enough for ordination by the time they commenced bachelor, of course. See Norman Sykes, *Church and State in England in the XVIIIth Century* (Cambridge, 1934), pp. 195–96. Waterland recognizes this fact and suggests that such students "proceed in Philosophical and Classical Learning" after taking their degrees and before proceeding to an intensive study of divinity (*Advice to a Young Student*, p. 28).

[4] See R. B. McDowell and D. A. Webb, "Courses and Teaching in Trinity College, Dublin, during the First 200 Years," *Hermathena*, LXIX (1947), 9–30. Also W. B. Stanford, "Classical Studies in Trinity College, Dublin, since the Foundation," *Hermathena*, LVII (1941), 3–24; J. E. L. Oulton, "The Study of Divinity in Trinity College, Dublin, since the Foundation," *Hermathena*, LVIII (1941), 3–29; E. J. Furlong, "The Study of Logic in Trinity College, Dublin," *Hermathena*, LX (1942), 38–53.

mained at Trinity the usual seven years, being "ready to take his degree of master of arts," Sir William Temple declared, "when he was forced away by the desertion of that College upon the calamities of the country" in 1689.[5] When he left Trinity in that year, at the age of twenty-one, he was still undecided whether to take orders and would, in any case, have to wait three more years for full orders. He tells us himself in the *Autobiographical Fragment* that as an undergraduate he "neglected some parts of his academick studies: for which he had no great relish by nature, and turned himself to reading history and poetry."[6] No mention is made of reading divinity, and, under the circumstances of his age and state of indecision, it is most unlikely that he undertook any such reading either as an undergraduate or, from the ages of eighteen to twenty-one, as a resident bachelor.

The years at Trinity, then, contributed very little, if anything, to the religious and philosophical materials which play so large a part in *A Tale of a Tub*. As far as the strictly religious materials of that book are concerned, Swift had not yet, in all probability, become acquainted with them through reading controversial divinity. With philosophical issues, on the other hand, he had ample opportunity and encouragement to become acquainted while at Trinity — at least within a strictly Aristotelian framework.[7] That he did not do so to any significant extent, however, nor with any close sympathy for the philosophical system to which he was exposed, is attested, not only by the distaste for such subjects which he expressed, but by the fact that they produced no appreciable effect on *A Tale of a Tub*. On the contrary, as we noticed in the last chapter, Swift's philosophical assumptions in his first book were assimilated at the same time and from the same sources as the conventions of Anglican religious controversy which he adopted. Swift's private reading for ordination, then, not his aca-

[5] *The Correspondence of Jonathan Swift*, ed. F. Elrington Ball (London, 1910), I, 2.

[6] Deane Swift, *An Essay upon the Life, Writings, and Character, of Dr. Jonathan Swift* (London, 1755), "The Appendix: The Family of Swift," p. 40.

[7] For a very good discussion of the philosophical atmosphere at Trinity in Swift's day and of the radical change in this atmosphere which had taken place by the time that Berkeley matriculated in 1700, see Emile Pons, *Swift: les anneés de jeunesse et le "Conte du tonneau"* (Strasbourg and London, 1925), pp. 122–32.

demic studies at Trinity, is the source to which we must look for the philosophical premises which Swift expresses in *A Tale of a Tub* as well as for the religious conventions which he puts to use there.

We can, I think, assume that Swift's reading for ordination took place after he left Trinity and, for the most part at least, after he decided to take orders. Certainly he showed no inclination for reading much divinity during most periods of his life, and it was probably the necessity for passing a fairly rigorous examination on this subject that was responsible for his extensive acquaintance with the religious materials which went into the writing of *A Tale of a Tub*. The list of his reading which he kept in 1697 and 1698, after he was safely ordained, contains the barest minimum of religious works and testifies to that continued preference for reading history and poetry which he had first expressed at Trinity.[8]

Swift seems to have decided upon taking orders in late 1691 or early 1692, at about the time he began his second residence with Temple. He had been thinking of this step for some time, of course, but as late as 1690 he was still undecided.[9] In a letter of February 11, 1692, Swift wrote that he was beginning "to think of entering into the Church."[10] His decision about this time to go up to Oxford to take the M.A. for which he had already qualified himself before leaving Trinity was apparently connected with his determination to take orders and was the earliest overt sign of this determination. Deane Swift wrote of this step: "I am inclined to believe that Dr. Swift's resolution of taking his master's degree was occasioned by a sudden impulse of the mind upon his first determination of going into the church."[11] During the spring of 1692, he was busy reviewing his classical and philosophical studies in preparation for his prelections. On May 3d he wrote his cousin: "I have got up my Latin pretty well, and am getting up my Greek," and he went on to express that distaste for reviewing "causes of Philosophy" which I have already quoted.[12] In the summer he

---

[8] The list is reprinted by Guthkelch and Nichol Smith in their edition of *A Tale of a Tub* (2d ed.; Oxford, 1958), pp. lvi–lvii.

[9] See the excellent discussion of this whole question by Louis A. Landa, *Swift and the Church of Ireland* (Oxford, 1954), pp. 1–5.

[10] *Correspondence*, I, 5.

[11] *Essay*, p. 45.

[12] *Correspondence*, I, 366.

took his M.A., and by November of 1692 he was writing of his ordination as a matter definitely decided upon.[13]

If Swift's reading of religious polemics only began upon his deciding to take orders, then, it cannot have started much before the opening of 1692. The only evidence of such reading which we possess, in fact, earlier than *A Tale of a Tub* itself appears in his *Ode to the Athenian Society*, which, on the testimony of its dedication, was written in January and February of 1692, at the very time Swift was making up his mind to be ordained. In this poem, he reproduces the conventional denunciations of sensationalism (Stanza IV), Epicurean cosmology (Stanza V), and speculative atheism in general (Stanzas VIII and IX), subjects which were apparently fresh in his head from some recent reading of religious apologetics against atheism. Yet it is fairly certain that he had completed most of his reading for ordination by the time he left Temple in May, 1694. Although he was not ordained until the following January, he was writing on June 3, 1694, that "I design to be ordained September next," and between June and September he could scarcely have done more than review his reading.[14] The unexpected delay in the accomplishment of his designs was due to the necessity of obtaining a testimonium from Temple, not to any lack of preparation.

It was presumably, then, between 1692 and 1694 that Swift carried on most of his reading for ordination, probably between his return from Oxford in the middle of 1692 and his departure from Moor Park in the middle of 1694. Although the *Ode to the Athenian Society* shows that he had begun some of this reading a little earlier, probably toward the end of 1691, his attention to reviewing his academic subjects before going up to Oxford would have precluded much reading in divinity before his return, and it is from the very time of Swift's taking up residence at Moor Park again, after taking his M.A., that Delany dated the beginning of that avid study for eight hours a day during the next seven years for which he claimed Swift's own testimony.[15] It is an interesting fact

[13] See *ibid.*, I, 10.

[14] *Ibid.*, I, 12.

[15] See Patrick Delany, *Observations upon Lord Orrery's Remarks on the Life and Writings of Dr. Jonathan Swift* (London, 1754), p. 50. Deane Swift, however, argues that Swift's intensive habits of study dated from his leaving Trinity (*Essay*, pp. 271–72).

also that Swift ceased the writing of his early odes at about this time and did not return to poetic composition until the end of 1693. The last of these early odes, the *Ode to Dr. William Sancroft*, he mentions in his letter of May 3, 1692, written when he was reviewing his academic studies.[16] The next of his poems which is extant, *To Mr. Congreve*, was not written until November, 1693. We may presume that between these dates, and through the spring of 1694, Swift was devoting, for the first and perhaps the last time in his life, a good part of his many hours of intensive study to the kind of reading necessary for ordination. In his letter to Winder of January 13, 1699, to which I have referred in chapter iii, Swift is solicitous for the return not only of the books which he had left at Kilroot but also of his papers, which included his "abstracts and collections from reading." [17] Some of these may very well have been those abridgments of sermons and religious discourses which those who were reading for ordination were strongly recommended to draw up and which the young newly ordained clergyman had brought with him to his first parish.

Such intensive study as this was necessary for the candidate for ordination, since the examination which he must pass in order to qualify for orders was fairly rigorous. This examination, which could be both oral and written, was conducted usually by the bishop who was to ordain, assisted by some of his chaplains and canons. The subjects covered were Greek, Latin, and the "parts of divinity." Candidates being examined on divinity were expected to be able to answer questions relating to Scripture, the Creed, the Thirty-nine Articles, and doctrinal differences between the Church of England and other Christian communions, as well as to defend the tenets of Christianity.[18]

A representative collection of sermons could provide useful prolegomena to all these subjects, and, as we have seen, candidates for ordination were advised to begin with them. They then proceeded to the reading of Scripture, various biblical exegeses, some of the classic commentaries on the Creed and the Thirty-nine Articles (such as Bishop Pearson's *Exposition of the Creed*), ec-

[16] *Correspondence*, I, 363.
[17] *Ibid.*, I, 30.
[18] For the manner of conducting ordination examinations and the subjects covered, see Sykes, *Church and State*, pp. 105–10.

clesiastical history, and, finally, some of the classics of religious controversy.[19]

The subject with which this last class of books dealt — polemical or controversial divinity — was regarded as particularly important. "Polemical or controversial divinity," Bishop Bull reminded his clergy in a visitation sermon preached between 1705 and 1710, "is *theologia armata*, or that part of divinity which instructs and furnisheth a man with necessary weapons to defend the truth against its enemies"; and he went on to stress the necessity of its study by every clergyman.[20] To this classification, of course, belong all those sermons and discourses of the Anglican rationalists against Catholicism, Puritanism, and atheism which we have seen to have played so important a part in the writing of *A Tale of a Tub*. We see now that it was highly probable that Swift should have been reading works of this kind during the three year period before he began to write his religious satire. It only remains to consider whether his choice of authors was eccentric in view of the change in the climate of apologetics that was taking place at the very time that he was reading controversial divinity.

Very interesting light on this question is provided in a little book by one of the principal targets of Swift's satire against abuses in learning, with whose views on religious matters, however, Swift never expressed any dissent. *Some Thoughts concerning a Proper Method of Studying Divinity* was written by William Wotton at some time, internal evidence shows, before 1718, at a period when the change in Anglican apologetics had already taken place and when religious polemics consisted principally of rejoinders to the deists and of elaborations of the argument from design against atheism by prominent physico-theologians. The list of reading which Wotton recommends to students of divinity suggests that if Anglican rationalism was no longer a living force in religious apologetics after the close of the Restoration era, some of the writings which it produced were still being read, though not always for the reasons which their authors had intended.

Wotton divides the study of divinity into four parts. One part

[19] See, for example, the general prospectus outlined in Waterland, *Advice to a Young Student*, pp. 16–17.
[20] *The Works of George Bull, D. D., Lord Bishop of St. David's*, ed. Edward Burton (Oxford, 1846), I, 146.

consists of Scripture along with numerous commentaries upon it, another of "systems of divinity," such as Pearson's *Exposition of the Creed* and Burnet's *Exposition of the Thirty-nine Articles* (1699). A third part consists of controversial divinity, which includes the Fathers, for their polemics against early heresies, and English apologists, for their attacks upon modern enemies of the church.

> An *English* Divine [Wotton points out] is obliged to preach to the People of *England*, and to defend the Faith and Discipline of the Church of *England* against all Opposers. The Manner of our preaching now, which is come to an admirable height, is chiefly to be learnt from the Preachers since the Restoration of King *Charles* II. and among them Archbishop *Tillotson* is unquestionably the greatest Man in that Way.[21]

Turning from sermons to more lengthy treatises, Wotton takes up the fourth and last part of divinity, which consists of polemical discourses against the modern enemies of the church. "The chief Enemies whom we have to oppose," he writes, "are *Papists, Dissenters, Arians,* and those whom we commonly call *Deists.*" He then proceeds to name some of the principal classics of controversy against each of these enemies which the student of divinity ought to read. He names nine books against the Catholics, two of which are Tillotson's *Rule of Faith* and Stillingfleet's *Rational Account of the Grounds of Protestant Religion.* The fact that every one of these nine books was written before 1690 simply underlines the rapid decline of anti-Catholic apologetics following the Revolution. Among books against the Protestant dissenters, Wotton gives first importance, as we might expect, to Hooker's *Laws.* It is when he takes up polemical discourses against the final class of enemies that the shift in apologetics becomes most noticeable. "Against those that deny either the Existence of God, or any actual Revelation of his Will to Mankind," he remarks, "this Age has produced more excellent Writers, than all the Ages that have gone before us." He names a number of the more recent physico-theologians,

[21] William Wotton, *Some Thoughts concerning a Proper Method of Studying Divinity* (London, 1734), pp. 14–15. Waterland likewise testifies to Tillotson's continued popularity. He advises the candidate for ordination to devote an entire year to the reading of Tillotson's sermons exclusively.

particularly some of the most famous Boyle lecturers, and recommends them for their arguments. Yet the Anglican rationalist discourses against atheism are still useful, for a different purpose. "The Opinions of the ancient Philosophers upon this Subject are very accurately described and explained by Dr. *Cudworth* in his [*True*] *Intellectual System of the Universe*," while "Bishop *Stillingfleet's Origines Sacrae*" will be found to "contain great Variety of useful and curious Learning upon these Heads." [22] Thus Cudworth and Stillingfleet have survived, not because their once famous books contain telling arguments, but because of the encyclopedic information to be found in their works.

The position which the writings of the Anglican rationalists still retained as classics of religious controversy at the beginning of the eighteenth century, then, makes it understandable that Swift should have become well acquainted with them in the course of reading for ordination. That he should have read their polemics against the Catholics or such attacks upon Puritanism as Hooker's *Laws* was a matter of course. And his reading of, and sympathy for, the Anglican rationalist apologetics against atheism seems almost as much a matter of course when we remember that it was between 1691 and 1694 that most of this reading probably took place. Although the arguments of the physico-theologians against atheism had been competing for some years with the Anglican rationalist discourses on the same subject, the ultimate triumph of the former and their success in driving their competitors from the field really dates from the inauguration of the Boyle lectures in 1692 by Wotton's friend Bentley. That the young man reading for ordination in Temple's library at Moor Park should have been completely *au courant* and aware of new trends in religious controversy is hardly to be expected. The religious satire which he wrote a few years later offers ample evidence that it was not merely as encyclopedias of "useful and curious learning" that he read the Anglican rationalist apologetics against atheism.

This, then, was a great part, at least, of the "Reading fresh in his Head" which Swift tells us, in the "Apology" to *A Tale of a Tub*, he had brought to the writing of his satire against abuses in religion. That his decision to write such a satire was occasioned by the same course of reading in religious controversy as provided

[22] *Some Thoughts*, pp. 17–19.

him with the materials for his book appears equally probable. "I look upon myself, in the capacity of a clergyman," he wrote in his "Thoughts on Religion," "to be one appointed by providence for defending a post assigned me, and for gaining over as many enemies as I can" (IX, 262). To the newly ordained clergyman with plenty of leisure on his hands in his first parish, the most effective means of exercising this capacity, suitable to his own talents, was to turn to account the materials of religious controversy with which he had recently become acquainted.

Fortunately, Swift's peculiar talents lay in satire, not in religious discourse, and "he resolved to proceed in a manner, that should be altogether new, the World having been already too long nauseated with endless Repetitions upon every Subject" (I, 1). The new manner which he chose was "to laugh at those Corruptions in Religion" which "all Church of *England* Men agree in." If this manner was different from that which the Anglican apologists whom he had been reading had used, his motive, nevertheless, was not essentially different from theirs. To expose the abuses in religion "in the most ridiculous Manner," he suggested in the "Apology," "is perhaps the most probable way to cure them, or at least to hinder them from farther spreading" (I, 2). That Swift's contemporaries in the church did not agree with this hopeful suggestion is notorious. But another of Swift's judgments of *A Tale of a Tub* has proven more accurate. He remarked that "the Book seems calculated to live at least as long as our Language, and our Tast admit no great Alterations." That this has proven to be the case is due, not to the long-forgotten materials from which he fashioned his book, but to the new and original uses to which he put them.

INDEX

Act of Uniformity, 70
Advice to a Young Student (Waterland), 155
Aeolists, 59–60, 63–68, 77–78, 115–17, 125
Agnosticism, philosophical, 50, 126–27, 138–39
Alexander the Great, 103
Anatomy of Melancholy (Burton), 105, 107, 113–16
Anaxagoras, 77
Anaximenes, 66–67, 87, 115
Anglican rationalists: apologetics of, 34–36; on atheists as enthusiastic madmen, 78–80, 82, 93–95; on the Catholics, 36–41, 43–45; compared with Hooker, 31–32; on the consensus gentium, 129–31; continued popularity of, 162–63; contrasted with Hooker, 47–48, 152; debt to Descartes, 146–51; decline of, 51, 151–53; defenses of, 30–31; on distinction between leaders and followers, 116–17; on distinction between madness and enthusiasm, 104–105; on enthusiasm as a product of the imagination, 122–27; on enthusiasm as religious melancholy, 105–11; on identity between science and faith, 43–45, 47–51; misconceptions concerning, 20–21; position on grounds of religion, 23–24; on proselytizing, 98–100; on the Puritans as enthusiastic madmen, 68–74; on sensationalism, 137–41; Swift's acquaintance with, 52–56; sympathy with the Royal Society, 90–92; theory of knowledge of, 143–53

Anima Magica Abscondita (Vaughan), 54, 60
Anselm, St., 51
Anthroposophia Theomagica (Vaughan), 54, 60
Antidote against Atheism, An (More), 36, 78–79, 148
Apollonius of Tyana, 86–87, 97
Aristotle: cosmology of, 89, 93; Glanvill's attack on, 53; in *Gulliver's Travels*, 153; philosophy of, studied at Trinity College, 156–57
Atheism, 23, 35–36, 49, 78–80, 89, 99, 111–12, 127, 137–43, 145, 153, 159, 163; *see also* Atheistic cosmologies, Atheistic enthusiasm, Materialism, Sensationalism
Atheistic cosmologies, 86–98, 125–27, 130–32, 153, 159
Atheistic enthusiasm, 78–80, 82, 85–90, 93–100, 111–12
Augustine, St., 51, 83

Baker, Thomas, 23 (n. 8)
Ball, F. Elrington, 53 (n. 1), 157 (n. 5)
Baxter, Richard, 23
Belief; *see* Faith
Bentley, Richard, 7, 163
Berkeley, George, 157 (n. 7)
Bethell, S. L., 20 (n. 4)
Boyle, Robert, 91–92
Boyle lectures, 23, 163
Bredvold, Louis I., 47 (n. 48)
Bull, George, 161
Bullitt, John M., 56 (n. 4)
Burnet, Gilbert, 162
Burton, Edward, 161 (n. 20)
Burton, Robert, 70–71, 105–8, 110, 113–16

168

Method of Studying Divinity (Wotton), 161
Spirit, testimony of the, 27, 29
Stanford, W. B., 156 (n. 4)
Stanley, Thomas, 66–67, 87, 115
Starkman, Miriam K., 11 (n. 13), 64 (n. 14), 88 (n. 43)
Steffan, Truman Guy, 71 (n. 19)
Stillingfleet, Edward, 20, 35, 54–55, 150, 162–63; adopts new apologetics, 152–53; attacks deism, 22 (n. 7), 32; attacks Epicurean and Cartesian cosmologies, 93; Cartesian influence on, 148; on Epicurean cosmology, 89–90; on identity of faith with science, 49–50; on rational criteria for faith, 45; on rational faith, 43; on sensationalism, 139–41
Supernatural religion, 26, 32–34, 36, 41, 47
Swift, Deane, 157 (n. 6), 158, 159 (n. 15)
Swift, Jonathan: acquaintance with the Anglican rationalists, 52–56; decision to take orders, 158–59; epistemological premises, 137–51; literary activities at Moor Park and Kilroot, 7–10; motive in beginning *A Tale of a Tub*, 163–64; on natural religion, 32–34; on private judgment, 128–30; reading of, for ordination, 159–64; on the reasonableness of mysteries, 46–47; studies at Trinity College, 155–57
Argument against Abolishing Christianity, An, 56
Autobiographical Fragment, 157
Battle of the Books, The, 11 (n. 12), 53
Correspondence, 52–53, 66, 158–60
Discourse concerning the Mechanical Operation of the Spirit, A, 10, 74–75
Gulliver's Travels, 153
Letter to a Young Gentleman Lately Entered into Holy Orders, A, 32–34, 55, 117
Mr. Collins's Discourse of Free-Thinking, 55–56
Ode to the Athenian Society, 159
Ode to Dr. William Sancroft, 160

Preface to the . . . Bishop of Sarum's Introduction, 16 (n. 1)
Remarks upon a Book Intitled "The Rights of the Christian Church," 55, 142
Sentiments of a Church-of-England Man, The, 128–29
Sermons, 46–47, 98–100, 129–30
Some Thoughts on Free-Thinking, 100
Tale of a Tub, A: basic satirical methods in, 4–6; dates of composition of, 6–10; immediate backgrounds of, 10–12; origin of, 154–64; parable of the three brothers in, 13–19, 29–30, 40, 45–46, 56–58, 77; purpose and arrangement of, 2–4; *see also* Aeolists, Parody, Tailor-worshippers. *Sections*: "Apology," 2–3, 6–7, 10–12, 163–64; II, 14–15, 75–78, 80, 82–85, 141–42; IV, 15–16; VI, 16–17, 29–30, 58–59; VIII, 59–60, 63–67, 78, 115–17, 125; IX, "Digression concerning Madness," 3–4, 9–10, 67–68, 85–89, 94–98, 101–3, 111–14, 117–22, 126–28, 131–37, 142–43; XI, 17, 68
Thoughts on Religion, 46, 164
To Mr. Congreve, 160
Sykes, Norman, 156 (n. 3), 160 (n. 18)
Sympathy, secret necessary, 118–20
Systems, reductive; *see* Reductive systems

Tailor-worshippers, 75–78, 80, 82–85, 141–42
Tatler, 55
Tavard, George H., 37 (n. 30)
Temple, Sir William, 7–8, 10–11, 52, 53 (n. 2), 154, 157–59, 163
Testimony of the Spirit, 27, 29
Thales, 66
Theologism, 51
Theory of knowledge; *see* Epistemology
Thirty-nine Articles, 160, 162
Thomas Aquinas, St., 23, 25 (n. 13, 14), 26 (n. 15, 16), 27 (n. 18), 41 (n. 36), 83

Tillotson, John, 20, 36–40, 55–57, 162; on atheism, 99, 116–17, 127, 131; on Epicurean cosmology, 89; on the grounds of religion, 32; on Hobbes, 81; on identity of faith with science, 48–49; on rational criteria for faith, 44–46; on religious fanaticism, 130; on the rule of faith, 36–40; on sensationalism, 140; on the soul, 80–81
Tindal, Matthew, 55
Tradition, 15–16, 37–40
Treatise concerning Enthusiasme, A (Casaubon), 72, 107
Trent, Council of, 37 (n. 30)
Trinity College, Dublin, 154–58
True Intellectual System of the Universe, The (Cudworth), 36, 55, 78–79, 148, 163
Tuveson, Ernest, 21 (n. 5), 56 (n. 4)

Understanding, common, 123–33, 136
Uniformity, Act of, 70

Vanity of Dogmatizing, The (Glanvill), 53

Vapors, 102–3, 108–15
Vaughan, Henry, 60
Vaughan, Thomas, 54, 60–61, 63, 68, 74, 94

Warly, John, 22 (n. 8)
Waterland, Daniel, 155, 156 (n. 3), 161 (n. 19), 162 (n. 21)
Webb, D. A., 156 (n. 4)
Webster, C. M., 70–71
Webster, John, 118–19
Westfall, Richard S., 24 (n. 11)
Wilkins, John, 23, 145, 153
Willey, Basil, 20 (n. 4)
Williams, Kathleen, 21, 56 (n. 4)
Williamson, George, 71 (n. 19)
Wilson, Thomas, 155–56
Winder, John, 52–53, 160
Wotton, William: charges Swift with impiety, 12; on the preparation of candidates for ordination, 161–63; quarrel with Temple, 10, 154

Yolton, John W., 152 (n. 55)

Zeal; *see* Enthusiasm, Puritanism